LACE
IDENTIFICATION
a practical guide

LACE
IDENTIFICATION
a practical guide

GILIAN DYE and JEAN LEADER

The Crowood Press

First published in 2021 by
The Crowood Press Ltd
Ramsbury, Marlborough
Wiltshire SN8 2HR

enquiries@crowood.com
www.crowood.com

British Library Cataloguing-in-Publication Data
A catalogue record for this book is available from the British
Library.

ISBN 978 1 78500 866 5

Acknowledgments
This book would not have happened without the help of our families and friends who have supported us over many years,
providing encouragement, examples for the illustrations and assisting with dating and other research. Particular thanks go to
Barbara and Tony Tapper, Barbara Pannel, Adrienne Thunder and Susan Wallace for substantial donations to our collections.
Also to the lace volunteers at the Discovery Museum in Newcastle (Jo Davis, Ann Hotchkiss, Karin Jackson and Val Lloyd) for
creative discussions.
We are also very grateful to the teachers who have passed on their technical lacemaking skills and historical knowledge, the
students who have asked difficult questions and curators and others who have provided access to lace collections large and
small.

Front cover: A long stole of Carrickmacross lace, probably made at the end of the nineteenth or beginning of the twentieth
century. The many shamrocks in this beautifully designed piece confirm the Irish origins. Other typical Carrickmacross features
are the scattering of little dots (known as pops) across the background, the loops of thread around the outer edge and the
spaces with decorative fillings.

Cover design: Design Deluxe

Frontispiece: Stole of Brussels Application lace.

Typeset by Derek Doyle & Associates, Shaw Heath
Printed and bound in India by Parksons Graphics Pvt Ltd., Mumbai.

CONTENTS

Four weeks after we agreed to write this book, Gil's sister Barbara handed her a small cardboard box labelled 'Narrow Lace Pieces'. The box, packed tight with lace, had been unopened since it came to her from her husband's grandmother, Mrs Maud Tapper, who had married the Rev. Martin Tapper in June 1901. At the top of the box was a rather crumpled length of bobbin lace with a machine lace edging and below that a fine crochet cuff mounted on net. Looking a little deeper it was clear that the box held exactly the sort of small lace pieces that the wife of a country parson could have used and re-used at the beginning of the twentieth century, examples that we might want to include in a reference book of everyday laces. This picture includes many of the edgings and insertions from the box.

INTRODUCTION

Lace is part of our lives and has been for generations, from underwear to high fashion, from cathedral vestments to cottage tablecloths. Lacemaking began in Europe in the sixteenth century, the main techniques being needle lace (developed from cutwork embroidery) and bobbin lace (evolving from surface braids). The thread used was usually linen – occasionally silk or precious metal. During the seventeenth and eighteenth centuries lace became more varied and worn extensively by both men and women in the higher levels of society: it was an expensive commodity.

Early in the 1800s there was a transition from lace being accessible only to the wealthy, to lace finding a place in the wardrobes and homes of a growing and increasingly affluent middle class. This was helped by the lowering of prices as a result of the Industrial Revolution: first came machine-made net to serve as a basis for handwork, and then machine-made imitations of handmade lace. Middle-class women had more leisure time, and crafts such as crochet and tatting became extremely popular.

The twentieth century saw the demise of handmade lace as an industry, although the last fifty years have seen a revival of lacemaking as a recreational pursuit. More recently there has been increasing interest in working in colour and non-traditional materials, in addition to traditional white lace worked in linen or cotton thread. While many lacemakers still enjoy the challenge of interpreting traditional patterns, others are using lace techniques for pictures, hangings and three-dimensional objects. Some of these items might not be immediately recognizable as lace, but a closer look will reveal the centuries-old techniques.

Most lace purchased new today is machine made, but large amounts of older lace can be found tucked away in drawers and boxes, or on sale at vintage fairs or other second-hand outlets. Some of this lace will also be machine made, but much will have been made by hand using a variety of techniques.

This book started life as a straightforward guide to the laces of the past 200 years. Not the top-of-the-range seventeenth-century exhibition pieces held in the major textile and costume collections, but the sort of lace that is likely to be treasured as a family heirloom, find its way into a local non-specialist museum or turn up in a charity shop. As the material came together we realized that it would be helpful to put the lace into context – social, domestic and commercial – so this is what we have tried to do.

Most of the illustrations are of items in the authors' collections. Neither of us is an active collector; occasionally we buy interesting pieces, but many items have been gifts from people who are keen to pass on lace that they know will be cared for and shared with others on a formal or informal basis. Our thanks go to these people, many now anonymous, and to the friends and relatives who have allowed us to include illustrations of their lace.

We hope this book will be of interest and help to collectors, to those trying to make sense of lace they have inherited or are sorting for a charity, and to museum staff who have no specialist textile background, but need to understand the lace in their stores before they can make it available and accurately labelled for their visitors.

A nineteenth-century collar which combines bobbin and needle lace. The central panel (the back of the collar) is needle lace with flowers and leaves of closely worked stitches set in a background of open mesh. At each side of the collar is a row of four small circles that are also needle lace. The woven look of motifs in the rest of the collar indicates that these are bobbin lace.

CHAPTER 1

TYPES OF LACE
AND MATERIALS

Needle lace and bobbin lace are the two classic laces, sometimes considered the 'real' laces. Needle lace is a form of free embroidery, made with a needle and a single thread. In contrast, bobbin lace is more like plaiting or weaving, made by manipulating multiple threads, each wound on a separate handle known as a bobbin. Both bobbin and needle lace evolved during the 1500s and many distinct styles have emerged over the succeeding centuries (see Chapters 3, 4, 5 and 6).

Other types of handmade lace are often described as craft laces. Some of these have been worked commercially, but most of the pieces you find will have been made in the home. Knitting and crochet are the most widely practised forms of craft laces (Chapter 8).

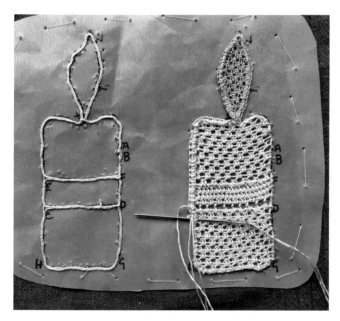

Working a needle lace motif. On the left a pattern has been tacked to a fabric backing, then two threads couched along the outline of the motif, with stitches going through both pattern and backing. On the right the motif has been filled with rows of buttonhole stitches, linked at each end of the row to the couched outline, but not going through the pattern. Additional threads laid over the couched outline are now being buttonhole stitched in place to give a raised outline and finish the lace. Once the stitching is complete the lace will be removed from the support by snipping the couching threads.

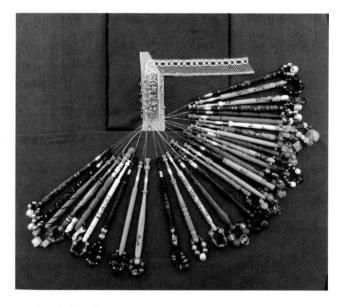

Working bobbin lace. A pattern, known as a pricking, is pinned to a firm pillow, then bobbins wound with thread are used two pairs at a time to work the stitches, which are held in place by pins placed in holes in the pricking. The lace being worked is an English bobbin lace known as Bucks Point.

Hand-knitted lace is worked in rows or rounds of interlinked loops using two or more needles and a single thread. This doily, worked in cotton, is typical of lace knitted in the home for domestic use. Knitted lace shawls, scarves and baby clothes have been worked both commercially and domestically in fine, soft wool.

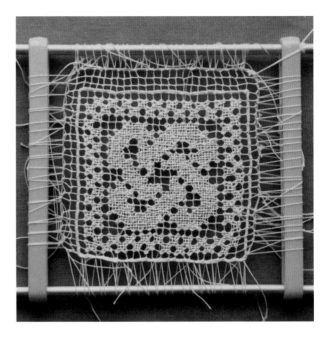

Filet (also known as lacis) is based on hand-knotted square-mesh net. In the earliest form designs are embroidered using a simple darning stitch. A greater variety of stitches were used when the craft was revived in the Victorian period. Stitching is easier when the net is stretched in a frame.

Crochet is worked with a single thread and a small hook. A basic looped stitch produces a simple chain; other stitches are built up with additional movements. Many crochet items are assembled from motifs; this example has nine flowers with four small connecting squares and a chain-stitch border with picots. Knitted lace is often finished with a similar crochet chain.

Tatting is a knotted lace worked with a small shuttle. Designs are composed mainly of rings and arcs, with picots that are both decorative and a means of linking different sections.

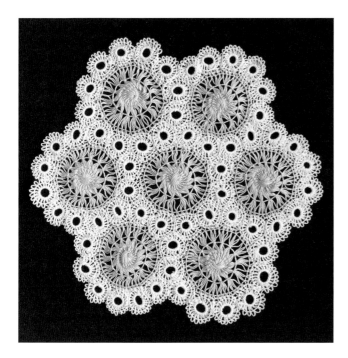

Tenerife lace is composed of linked needle-woven circles. The technique developed from a form of openwork embroidery known as sol lace. It is worked on a temporary support, such as a circle of pins on a pincushion.

Three examples of machine-made lace. The lace at the top has a mesh background and open-work areas which may give the appearance of handmade bobbin lace, but closer inspection shows rather muddled threads in the mesh and tightly packed threads in the more solid areas; these are typical of lace made on a Leavers machine. Lace worked on a Barmen machine can be more difficult to distinguish from handmade bobbin lace, but the extreme regularity of the repeats in the second lace gives a clue that this piece is also machine made. The fuzziness of the third lace gives it away as being chemical lace – worked by machine embroidering on a background that was then chemically dissolved away.

There are other forms of craft laces which are based on woven fabric or machine-made net, also various laces that combine two or more techniques, for example needle lace with machine-made tapes.

Experiments in using machines to make lace started towards the end of the eighteenth century and by 1809 it was possible to produce a hexagonal net that became the foundation for the wide variety of embroidered and appliquéd laces described in Chapter 7. Over the following decades machines were adapted to produce patterned nets. Then a stream of technical developments led to a variety of machines all aiming to copy existing lace or create new styles, to satisfy an ever-increasing demand for fashion and household fabrics (Chapter 9).

Making lace by hand continued alongside developments in machine lace until the end of the nineteenth century, by which time neither bobbin lace nor needle lace were commercially viable except at the very top end of the market. The small industries that produced knitted and crochet lace, or net- or fabric-based open work were also struggling, but many of these continued as domestic crafts until well into the twentieth century, enjoying intermittent revivals up to the present day. Machine lace had its ups and downs over the twentieth century, never completely losing its popularity for underwear and household furnishings, and now in the twenty-first century making considerable impact on the catwalks and in the online stores.

In Britain there was a great revival of interest in handmade lace in the 1960s and 70s with classes and new books, and a general mixing of ideas and techniques including use of coloured threads and non-traditional materials. Lacemaking has struggled in the twenty-first century, but there are signs that the internet may be helping to reverse this trend.

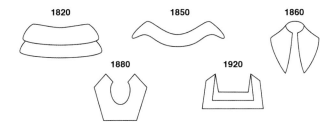

Sketches of collars taken from fashion plates and other sources where the date of a collar is known.

Dating lace

This is an area that is notoriously difficult. It is usually possible to give the earliest date that a particular type of lace was made, but similar lace may have been made at any time up to the present day and in any part of the world. Only on rare occasions will an item have a clear date provenance. Sometimes a knowledge of fashion history may help since the style of an item can give a clue to the age of the lace involved, but lace is a valuable fabric and often re-used, sometimes combining pieces of different types and ages – something that is not always obvious at first sight.

The focus for this book is lace that has been made since the end of the eighteenth century, the time when machine-made lace began to compete with handmade bobbin and needle lace. There is a time line at the end of the book that gives dates for the first appearance of certain laces and some of the social and other factors that influenced the making and wearing of lace.

Terminology

Lace has been made and used in many ways, in many places and over many hundreds of years, so it is not surprising that the terminology can be confusing. In the Glossary towards the end of this book we have given the meanings of specialist words we use.

Materials

Lace can be made with any material that can be cut, drawn or twisted into a thread. Most of the early lace was worked in linen (spun from flax). Coloured silk and metal threads were also used extensively for bobbin lace in the sixteenth and sev-

enteenth centuries. Delicate bobbin and needle laces made in the eighteenth century required exceptionally fine linen threads, the best being produced in Flanders. Cotton started to replace linen for working bobbin and needle laces in the middle of the nineteenth century.

Fine wool was the yarn of choice for knitted lace scarves and shawls in the nineteenth century, and wool and other natural fibres such as bamboo are now being used for bobbin lace scarves. Some of the heavier bobbin lace trimmings popular in the Victorian period were also worked in wool.

At the beginning of the nineteenth century, silk was the only fine thread available that was smooth and strong enough to cope with the stresses of working machine net and lace. A strong, smooth cotton thread became available around 1810 and was the yarn of choice for machine laces until synthetic threads took over in the 1950s.

It is sometimes possible to distinguish between cotton and linen by feel or looking at a thread under magnification – cotton threads are usually smooth, while linen threads have little bumps. Silk and artificial silk are difficult to distinguish by look and feel, but silk is an animal protein and artificial silk is plant-based cellulose so if you are prepared to sacrifice a small amount of thread, you can try a burning test – silk will smell like burning hair, artificial silk (rayon) like burning paper. For detailed information about the structure of threads see Pat Earnshaw's *Threads of Lace from Source to Sink*.

Today most machine lace is made with one of the many synthetic threads, or a blended yarn such as polyester and cotton, while a lacemaker might utilize anything from the traditional silk, linen and cotton threads to wire, found objects or strips of plastic.

Thread structure and thickness

Most bobbin laces and many early needle laces were made with 2-ply linen thread, occasionally silk, and later cotton thread was used. Some techniques, such as crochet, require a firmer, more rounded thread; this is usually achieved by twisting together three 2-ply threads. Synthetic threads are usually produced as continuous filaments, which are twisted to produce similar structures.

Stranded embroidery cotton (also known as embroidery floss) is not a traditional thread for making lace, but it is becoming increasingly popular for coloured lace and it is a thread that many people know, so we are mentioning it here as a rough guide to the thickness of threads used for making

lace. The majority of laces are made with threads that are in thickness between one and four strands of embroidery floss, but there are a number of machine nets and bobbin laces, such as Honiton, that are worked with finer threads.

Place of origin

Unless otherwise stated lace described here was originally made in Europe, but lacemaking has now spread worldwide, with numerous combinations of styles and techniques. Lace is often named after a location where it was made – Honiton, Bruges, Alençon and so on – but this defines neither where all lace of that name was made, nor the style of all lace made in that place.

Most 2-ply threads used by lacemakers are S-twist, so the line of the twist is in the same direction as the diagonal of a capital S – as in the example on the left. Twisting a group of S-twist threads together results in a Z-twist cord (on the right).

A group of machine and handmade laces showing a variety of styles and techniques.

APPROACHING AN IDENTIFICATION

Lace is a complicated subject. This is only to be expected with a fabric that has been made in the home with a pair of knitting needles or in a vast factory with complex machinery. It is a fabric that has adapted over five centuries to the vagaries of fashion and, in the past 200 years, to rapid developments of technology. This can make identification tricky and sometimes it is necessary to record an item as being 'x type' or 'probably y'. The good news is that certain types of lace turn up more frequently than others, and the common laces often have features that make them relatively easy to identify; some

Table prepared for a study session. In addition to the lace there is the lace identification app prepared by Jean and David Leader, tape measure, notebook and pencil, and two means of magnification – a magnifying glass and a Phonescope – all laid out on dark purple jersey fabric.

If no mannequin is available a polo-neck sweater on a padded hanger provides a useful substitute for viewing a collar.

examples are given later in this chapter. Also, the more lace you study, and preferably handle, the easier identification becomes. For study purposes small pieces, or those that are in poor repair, are often as interesting as larger items.

If you are working on the identification of a batch of laces then it is worth getting yourself organized. In a museum setting a curator's requirements would be that you wash your hands, remove jewellery and other items that might catch on the lace, avoid fluffy jumpers and keep food and drink well clear of your study area. This is good practice when working with your own collection. Obviously, it is not practical when rummaging through a box at a car boot sale; there you must trust your instincts and be prepared to pay a reasonable sum for a piece of interest that can be examined later at your leisure.

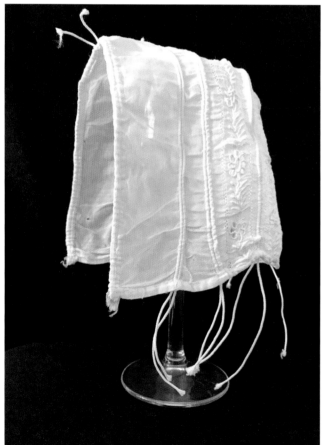

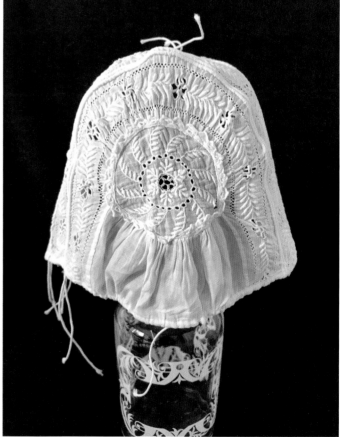

Putting a baby's bonnet on a large wine glass allows you to see its shape, and also in this example to see what appears to be a dirty mark on one corner – closer inspection shows that this is the remnant of a coloured ribbon. A coloured background is needed to show detail of stitching, which is provided in the second picture where a soft ball covered in dark green fabric has been balanced on a jar.

Ideally you will have good lighting, a dark background on which to view light-coloured lace and a light background for black lace. Some simple props for collars, bonnets and other three-dimensional items can be helpful.

Other useful items to have to hand include: notebook and pencil (avoid pens as they could mark the lace); reference book(s) and/or identification app; tape measure; magnifier. At one time we relied on a pocket magnifier (loupe) or linen tester to see the detail of lace stitches, these are still useful tools, but digital cameras on our phones or tablets can be equally helpful.

Start by looking at the whole piece. What is the overall shape – is it a complete item (for example a collar or table mat), a single repeat, a short or long length? Is it a border (edging) or an insertion? Look at it from different angles, and if it is an item such as a collar try to view it on an appropriate support. If it is your own lace you can try it on yourself or a friend, but this is not usually permitted in a museum – there you might have mannequins you can use. (Be aware that some mannequins are very strange shapes.)

A roll of coloured fabric slid inside a sleeve allows you to see the detail of stitches, while something as simple as a ball or pudding basin balanced on a jar allows you to see the way a bonnet would look in use. Be inventive in your choice of support, but also be careful so you don't damage the lace in any way by catching it on sharp edges or allowing dirt or colour to be transferred from the background.

Make a note of anything you know about the history of the piece, including when and where you acquired it – this is its provenance (preparing this book would have been a great deal easier if we had followed this advice twenty years ago!). However, be wary of family tradition unless you have documentary evidence – it is a real bonus when you can match up a piece of lace with a family photo.

Then look at the detail.

The relevance of the following questions will become clear as you read about the structure of different laces in the chapters that follow.

- Does the lace appear to be worked as a continuous piece or assembled from separate sections?
- Do the front and back look similar?
- Is there a net (mesh) background? If so, what shape is the mesh?
- Are there gaps between motifs that are crossed by connecting bars? Do the bars have decorative loops (picots)?
- Are there picots along the outside edge?

This bobbin lace edging is composed of separate motifs linked by bars decorated with the little loops known as picots, and there are also picots all along the lower edge. The strip along the top is of a different density worked with a different thread and almost certainly machine made. Borders, collars and other items often have a separate strip stitched along one edge, which is known as an engrelure and is there to protect a more valuable lace so it is not damaged when the lace is removed for washing or re-use.

A Phonescope is an inexpensive gadget that fits over the lens of a mobile phone and allows close-up photos to be taken – very helpful when studying background stitches. (Phonescopes can be found online and in museum shops and the larger garden centres.)

- Are all the threads the same thickness?
- Can you see a tape (braid) that meanders through the lace?
- Does the piece appear to have been altered in any way? Are there places where the lace is coming apart?
- Is the lace mainly composed of looped stitches?
- Is there anything that might make you think it is machine lace? A fuzziness? A ribbed effect? The same error on every repeat? Very wide pieces with no sign of a join?
- Is there a strip along one edge that looks very different from the rest?

After studying the overall look of a piece you may need a more detailed view of the structure before reaching a decision on identification; this is where magnification may be required.

Many laces are composed of relatively dense pattern areas – known as clothwork – set in a background mesh – known as a ground. Some types of lace have many varieties of ground; illustrations at the end of this chapter, all taken with a Phonescope attachment for a mobile phone, show a variety of hand- and machine-made stitches. There is also a page showing snapshots of nine common laces laces that you are likely to find in a general collection. Each lace is described in more detail in the relevant chapter. (Illustrations are not to scale.)

Record keeping

Once you start building up a collection it is a good idea to start an organized record of the lace you own. There are several ways to approach this. You might start with a notebook making notes on each of your pieces, perhaps a page per item, written as each piece is studied, but leaving space for additional information. The disadvantage of this approach is that as the collection becomes larger it will become more difficult to find individual records.

Using a loose-leaf file or a pack of index cards instead of a notebook will allow sorting of records into sections, for example according to type of lace (bobbin, needle, crochet, machine…) – or type of item (edging, doily, collar, undergarment…). Similar records can be kept electronically, either as simple Word documents, or in more specialist programs that will allow the use of key words to search the records – for example to find details of all your crochet collars.

The record cards shown both give the type of object and style of lace, together with the size and an indication of the lace's provenance. Both say when the lace was acquired, and both have space for adding additional information – either on the back of the card, or at the bottom of the page if this is an electronic record. This is the bare minimum of information to include. How much other information you record depends on the type of item, the size of the collection and how you expect to use it.

Lace Collection		
Location		
File	Identity no. 002	No. of items 1
Type Bobbin		Type Specific Mechlin
Item Edging		
Date 18th C	Colour	Material
Length 140 cm	Width 4 cm	
Features Flanders ground — half st without pin		
Condition	Valuation	Date
Related items		
Maker/Merchant	Designer	
Acquisition		
Source From Susan Wallace		Date July 2000
Provenance Brought from Germany by her aunt c 1938		
Recorder JL		Date 21/8/2002
Notes		

Embroidered linen cloth with bobbin lace at each end
30cm x 77cm
Lace 1cm wide with 3 cm repeat
Mid 17 C
Gift from Pat Rowley (Feb 2017) with her note:
A towel or napkin of about 1660 trimmed with bobbin lace that is probably English. Notice how similar the embroidered design is to patterns found on English samplers.

The two record cards show two different approaches to recording an item of lace. The one at the top uses a database program that could be used for museum records, with words in bold appearing on every card. The more informal approach of the second card might be more appropriate for a small personal collection.

RECORD CARDS – SOME SUGGESTIONS FOR HEADINGS

Location – where the lace is stored.

File – category of item, for example lace edging, pattern, bobbin, collar…

Identity number – any item accepted into a museum is given a unique 'accession number', for example 2020/009, which indicates that it is the ninth item acquired in the year 2020. This number would be recorded on the item's packaging and a label attached to the item itself.

No. of items – a pair of cuffs, for example, would be recorded as 2 (in this case they might have accession numbers 2020/012a and 2020/012b).

Date – there are four places on the card that ask for a date; the first is the date the item was made, the others are records of when things have happened within the collection.

Colour – most lace ranges in colour between bright white and coffee-coloured and experience has shown that it is virtually impossible to agree on names for the colours in between – white, off white, pale cream, ecru – especially as they can appear different in different lights, so keep it simple.

Material – usually cotton, linen or silk, occasionally metallic, wool or synthetic.

Condition – here you can note if the item is 'as new', or if it is badly stained or falling apart.

Valuation – it is unusual to be able to put anything in this section, but if you bought the item you could include that price.

Related items – might be pieces acquired from the same source, or similar items from a different source.

Maker/merchant – sometimes you will have information about the company or individual that made or sold the item.

Designer – this might be the same person as the maker for a recent piece.

Including a photograph with your record is relatively easy to do these days and it is often useful to show both detail and an overall image.

Notes on care of lace

TO WASH OR NOT TO WASH?

The general advice is not to wash any lace you acquire unless it is unpleasantly filthy, in which case first try soaking in several changes of lukewarm water – always supporting the wet lace as it is lifted in and out of the water. Gently remove excess moisture with a white towel, then ease the lace into shape and allow to dry on a clean, plastic-covered board. If for any reason you decide more cleaning is required, follow reputable modern advice such as can be found in the Resources section.

Use a specialist mild detergent – Orvus® is often suggested but there are others such as Dehypon® LS45 which is commonly used by British textile conservators. For coloured lace, or lace attached to coloured fabric, always check for colour fastness before washing.

Any lace that might contain moths or other insect pests, or their eggs, should be sealed in a plastic bag and placed in a freezer for at least a week before being allowed anywhere near the rest of your collection. All textiles are damaged by light, so keep lace out of strong sunlight and do not display any items for long periods.

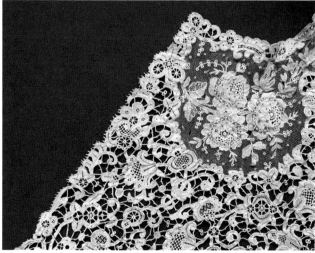

Today we expect commercial dyes to be colour-fast, but that has not always been the case and older fabrics can often transfer colour to adjacent materials. That is what has happened to the edge of a large needle lace collar that had been stitched to a length of purple fabric (upper image). Some of the dye has transferred to the lace, giving a distinctly mauve tinge. (This dye was possibly the dye invented accidentally by William Perkin in 1856, which was the first of the synthetic dyes to come into use. Perkin was only eighteen at the time and had been trying to synthesize quinine as a cure for malaria.) Several changes of lukewarm water over a period of two days and all trace of the dye has gone (lower image).

Not all stains can be removed in this way. The upper image shows a collar that was in a very sorry state when it was taken from the bottom of a carrier bag. The usual soaking in lukewarm water has freshened up the lace and revealed the full interest of a Point de Gaze collar. Unfortunately brown spots have remained, which are known as iron mould, and there is little that can be done to remove them without risking damage to the threads, so it is best not to try. (Note: the net under the lace has been used to take the weight of the collar as it was lifted in and out of the water.)

Storage

Store lace flat if possible, between sheets of acid-free tissue paper. Tissue paper must be acid-free, if it doesn't say on the packaging that it is acid-free it isn't, and will discolour your lace if used for long-term storage. Also never be tempted to use coloured tissue as the dye from this will leak at the slightest sign of moisture. Long lengths should be rolled around tissue-paper-covered tubes: wind the lace like a Swiss roll with a layer of tissue paper, continuing the paper to wrap the whole. Tape or ribbon tied in a bow can help to identify the contents without the need for unwrapping. (Elastic bands should not be used.) Where folds are necessary put a roll of tissue within the fold. Pad any three-dimensional item with tissue paper. Store in a box or drawer lined with tissue paper or other acid-free material, do not seal in a plastic bag or box.

Archival envelopes (also acid-free) are ideal for storing flat items. They come in several sizes and the most useful ones are transparent on one side and opaque on the other; this allows the contents to be seen without the need for unwrapping. There is a white acid-free fabric known as Tyvek that museums use for bags to contain costume and other large items; well-washed and rinsed sheeting is another option for wrapping large items. Wide, shallow drawers designed for storing maps and other large paper documents are also ideal for storing lace. They will take large items such as dresses encased in tissue paper or Tyvek bags, numerous collars stored flat between layers of tissue paper, or large numbers of smaller items with appropriate packing.

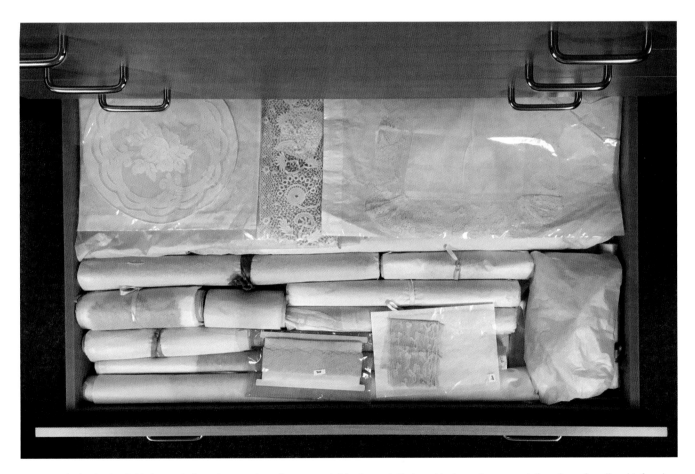

Towards the back of this large shallow drawer, three items are visible through their archival envelopes – a doily, a large handkerchief and some Irish crochet. In the front half of the drawer are a number of rolls of different lengths for edgings, insertions and larger items such as stoles. At centre front is a neat method of storing a long length of narrow lace: an H-shaped card, with a padded middle section on which the lace is wound, stored in a small archival envelope, and there is just room in the corner for a bonnet padded and wrapped with tissue paper.

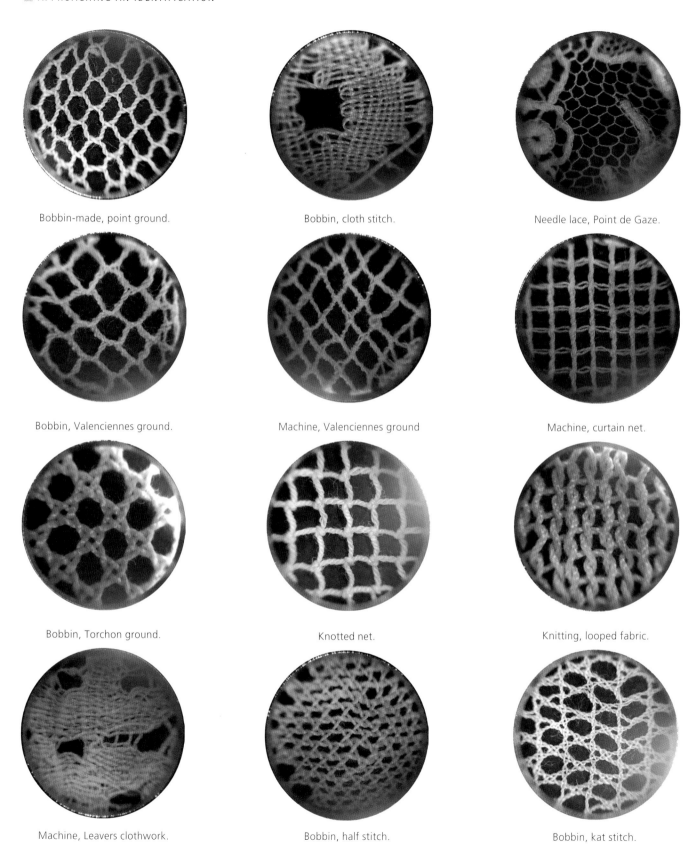

Bobbin-made, point ground.

Bobbin, cloth stitch.

Needle lace, Point de Gaze.

Bobbin, Valenciennes ground.

Machine, Valenciennes ground

Machine, curtain net.

Bobbin, Torchon ground.

Knotted net.

Knitting, looped fabric.

Machine, Leavers clothwork.

Bobbin, half stitch.

Bobbin, kat stitch.

A selection of lace stitches photographed with a Phonescope.

Maltese lace: bobbin lace always including a Maltese cross. Large collars and mats are common.

Princess lace: machine-made tapes hand stitched to machine net; often sold in souvenir shops.

Torchon: a geometric bobbin lace widely made by amateur and professional lacemakers.

Valenciennes: hand (top) and machine versions widely used to trim lingerie and baby clothes.

Carrickmacross: background of machine-made net with features of fine fabric appliqué.

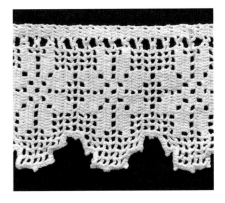

Filet crochet: frequently found as wide edgings on items such as table cloths and church linens.

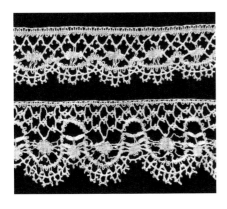

Bedfordshire: bobbin lace featuring plaits, picots and tallies, early twentieth-century examples.

Tatting: often found on collars and handkerchief edgings, featuring knotted rings and chains with picots.

Chemical lace: machine embroidered on a disposable background.

Nine Common Laces

Bobbin lace edgings with mesh ground: two of the laces are Torchon, three are point ground.

CHAPTER 3

CONTINUOUS BOBBIN LACE WITH MESH GROUNDS

Bobbin lace is worked with multiple threads, each wound on a separate handle known as a bobbin. Bobbins are used in pairs to work a wide variety of stitch combinations. Techniques evolved in the sixteenth century and fashion for bobbin lace spread rapidly across Europe, with local workshops springing up to meet the demand. Working is basically simple, involving the crossing of one thread from left to right between two pairs, and the twisting of threads within pairs from right to left, the result is somewhere between plaiting and weaving. As the work progresses pins are placed when there is a change of direction, to help with tension or provide the little loops known as picots.

There are many varieties of bobbin laces. For the purposes of this book we have separated them into three main groups.

Continuous laces are laces where most, if not all, the threads needed for the full width of the lace are hung on at the start and remain in use throughout, as the work continues in one direction. This group can be sub-divided into mesh-based laces (described in this chapter) and guipure laces with plaited grounds (Chapter 4). The continuous bobbin laces you are most likely to find are edgings and insertions. Wide pieces of continuous lace may require hundreds of threads and therefore hundreds of bobbins. The third group are the non-continuous laces; these can usually be worked with relatively few bobbins. Laces in this group include the pieced and braid laces which are described in Chapter 5.

Grounds

The term 'ground' is a name for the arrangement of stitches that forms the background around and between solid areas of a lace design. There are dozens of different grounds, some are very simple, composed entirely of one stitch repeated across the whole area, others are more complex groupings of four or more stitches arranged in specific ways. Different styles of lace have different grounds or a combination of grounds. Ground stitches may also be used as fillings in spaces within both non-continuous and continuous laces.

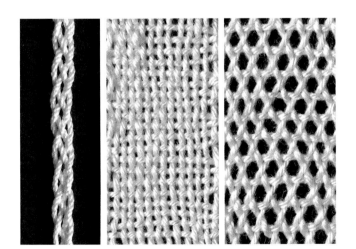

Two pairs make a plait (on left). Adding more pairs allows for a wide range of stitch combinations to be created including cloth stitch which looks like woven fabric (centre), and half stitch (on the right) which has diagonal threads. In addition there are numerous open stitches, known as 'grounds', which are illustrated later in this chapter.

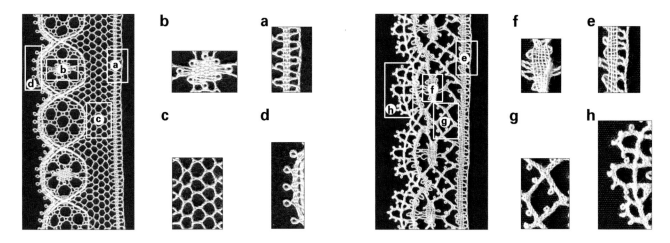

Continuous bobbin lace can be mesh-based (left) or guipure (right). These two edgings both have a straight edge on the right with some threads running vertically and others horizontally (**a** and **e**) – this edge is known as the footside. Both laces have areas of cloth stitch (**b** and **f**), and little loops where pins were placed to hold threads as the work progressed. The main difference is the contrast between the net ground (**c**) in the mesh-based edging, and the ground of plaits and picots (**g**) in the guipure edging. Both laces have picots on the scalloped left-hand edge – known as the headside – but the structure is different with a continuous line of picots along the headside of the mesh-based edging (**d**), while an arrangement of plaits with picots forms the headside of the guipure lace (**h**).

FOOTSIDES AND HEADSIDES

The two pieces of lace in the illustration above are both edgings, they each have a straight footside which will be stitched to the edge of fabric, and a shaped headside which will hang free. The detail of the ways headsides and footsides are worked varies between one lace tradition and another and can sometimes help distinguish where the lace was made.

Footsides for edgings are nearly always straight, while headsides can be shaped or straight. Lace with two straight footsides can be used as an insertion between two widths of fabric. Occasionally lace is made with two shaped headsides; this is either intended to be applied to the surface of fabric (when it might be referred to as a galloon) or used on its own, for example as a lappet, tie or garter.

Note: in most of the illustrations of edgings in this book the footside is shown at the top and the headside at the bottom, as this is the way the lace would hang in use.

The lace at the top has two straight edges, but the upper edge has picots, which could not be easily stitched to fabric. This indicates it is a headside, so the lace is an edging. The lace in the centre has two identical straight footsides, which would allow the lace to be stitched as an insertion between two widths of fabric. Both edges of the third lace are wavy headsides, which makes the lace suitable for surface decoration or to be used for something like a garter or tie.

Torchon

Torchon lace has a long history and is today one of the most popular laces for amateur lacemakers across the world. It is a geometric lace with a regular ground and a variety of cloth-stitch and half-stitch features. One of the strengths of Torchon is its versatility. It works well in colour and can be at any scale – worked with any yarn, from fine silk to marine cable.

Traditionally Torchon is worked on a regular grid with lines of stitches at 45 degrees to the footside, using white or ecru linen or cotton thread. However, there are numerous possi-

bilities with other yarns and grids and many lacemakers have been experimenting with these since the 1970s. For example, a 60-degree grid can be used for a circular or hexagonal motif, or part of a circular grid for a fan or collar, while fascinating effects can be achieved on a logarithmic grid, particularly when coloured threads are used.

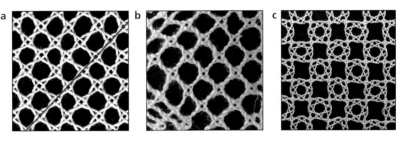

Torchon grounds
a is the basic Torchon ground. **b** is Dieppe ground, a variation of Torchon ground with an extra twist between the pins. **c** is one of many varieties of rose ground worked in units of four pins. The diagonal line shows the positioning of the pins as the lace was worked: this line is at 45 degrees to the direction of work – usually described as '45 degrees to the footside'. All three grounds were worked at this angle.

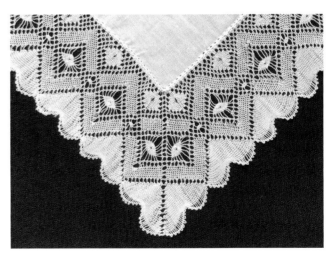

These two Torchon edgings show different interpretations of an almost identical pattern. Both edgings have the headside scallop known as a Spanish fan, and a standard Torchon footside. In the lower sample there are diamonds worked in half stitch between triangles of rose ground, while in the upper sample the diamonds are part half stitch and part cloth stitch, set in basic Torchon ground. There is a slight difference in width (2.25cm and 2.5cm) due to an extra row of pins and one extra pair in the lower sample.

For this handkerchief border a wide Torchon edging has been adapted to provide a neat corner – a twentieth-century innovation. The headside is formed from heart-shaped fans worked in cloth stitch, there are cloth-stitch diamonds with central holes, a small amount of Torchon ground near the footside, plus large spiders and V-shapes worked in half stitch. 4cm wide with 3cm repeat.

Putting together four corners makes a square. The square on the left is worked on a standard 45-degree grid; that on the right is on a logarithmic grid. Both use the same stitches and combination of coloured threads, but the effects are very different. Each square is 9.5cm × 9.5cm.

A 60-degree grid was used for the hexagonal motif, which was worked as six corners. The heart-shaped fans are structurally the same as those in the handkerchief on the previous page but the different angle and the use of a contrast colour give them a different look. The other features are rose ground and small half-stitch diamonds. Diameter 8.5cm.

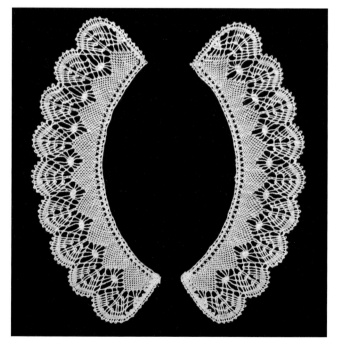

A two-part collar worked on sections of a curved grid. This has Spanish fans, spiders, and half stitch filling the space towards the footside. 6cm wide.

Patterns can also be reduced in size for dolls' houses including miniatures such as this Torchon owl, worked in fine silk – the frame is just 3cm across.

A Torchon variation was made in the village of 's Gravenmoer in the Netherlands from 1830 to 1914. The distinctive feature of 's Gravenmoer lace is the half stitch which has diagonal and vertical threads. This is unlike standard half stitch, which has diagonal and horizontal threads; instead it is close to the appearance of lace made on the Barmen machine. The lace was mainly used for the traditional lace caps of the area.

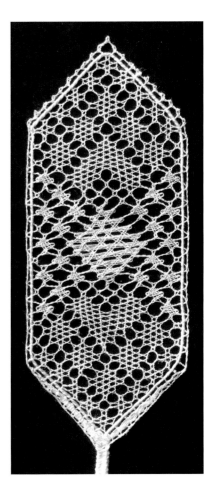

Torchon patterns can be easily enlarged for working with wool and other soft materials to make scarves. Some artists are going much larger, using 'threads' such as marine cable for architectural work.

Point Ground

Point ground, also known as Lille ground or tulle, is a lightweight hexagonal mesh which is relatively quick to work. Lace that features point ground can be found in most lacemaking traditions with other hexagonal mesh grounds and fillings also used in these laces. In 2001 *Point Ground, a Comparative Study* was published by OIDFA (an international lace organization); this is a book that shows in detail the similarities and differences of twenty-three point-ground laces from thirteen countries across Europe. Some of these laces are described here.

Bucks Point

Point-ground lace collected in the British Isles is most likely to have been made in Buckinghamshire or one of the neighbouring counties (Bedfordshire and Northamptonshire) where it was made commercially from the early 1800s to meet the need for delicate lace for the frills and flounces demanded by early nineteenth-century fashion. Unfortunately for lacemakers, point ground was relatively easy to copy on the early lace machines.

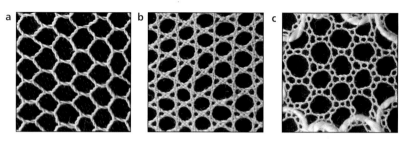

Grounds with hexagonal mesh

a is point ground: at the top and bottom of each hexagon two threads cross left over right, on each of the other four sides there are two threads twisted three times. **b** is kat stitch (also known as Paris or wire ground); in this the hexagon is defined by twisted threads, two pairs running vertically, and pairs from each side travelling diagonally. **c** is honeycomb, which is hexagonal in construction although the holes often appear circular. The angle to the footside of most hexagonal grounds is between 52 and 72 degrees, with 60 degrees being usual for circular and hexagonal mats and motifs.

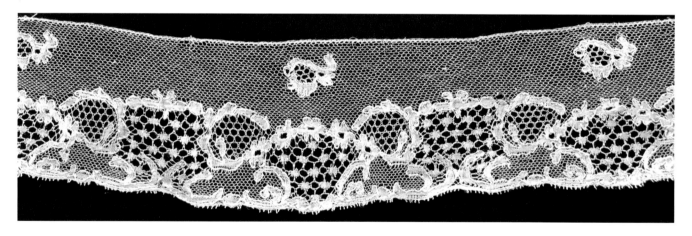

A 6cm wide Bucks Point border; it is 96cm long and joined into a circle, which indicates it was once part of a sleeve flounce. The lace has a number of typical Bucks Point features including the picots along the headside and a wide area of point ground, which would have allowed this lace to gather easily. The decoration on the lower half consists of open shapes (known as caskets) bounded by cloth stitch, with outlines of a thicker thread, known as a gimp. The caskets near the headside have fillings of point ground, while the larger caskets have a filling known as 'old mayflower'; the filling for the other areas is honeycomb stitch.

The ground for this lace is kat stitch decorated with small flower motifs; below that is a row of pear shapes enclosing fillings of point ground with square tallies, the headside has a row of tiny flowers. Each motif is outlined with a gimp thread. The amount of patterning towards the footside means this lace does not gather as easily as the one above so is more likely to have been used almost flat.

TALLIES

Tallies are small, dense areas formed by weaving one thread from side to side over three (or more) other threads. These blocks are found mainly in bobbin lace, in a variety of shapes, and are often called by local names – for clarity the name 'tally' is used throughout this book.

Fat, often almost round tallies, found in good Maltese.

Square-ended tallies, known as wheatears, found in early Bedfordshire.

Pointed tallies (leaves) found in Cluny and later Bedfordshire.

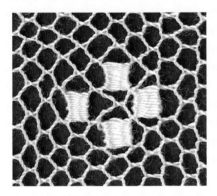

Bucks Point tallies are usually square, called *point d'esprit* when dotted through the ground.

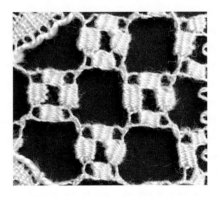

Tallies in Honiton are called leadworks; they are also square and usually found in groups.

Rectangular tallies, known as cucumber tallies, are worked with pairs from each side of a space.

Other Point-Ground Laces

During the nineteenth century point-ground laces were made in most European countries, and in England there were several small industries in addition to those in the East Midlands. These included Malmesbury and Downton in Wiltshire, Eye in Suffolk and the area around Honiton in Devon (where it was known as trolly lace). Designs of all English point grounds were influenced by imported examples from Europe and there was considerable overlap in design between laces from the different industries, but there are a few patterns which seem to have been specific to one area – if you have reason to believe that you are looking at one of these then it would be worth seeking out the appropriate book in the Resources section.

Tønder

This is a nineteenth-century point-ground lace made first in the Danish town of Tønder close to the German border. The thread used is often finer than that used for other point-ground laces giving a more fragile look to the background. In contrast the gimps that outline the motifs may be relatively dominant.

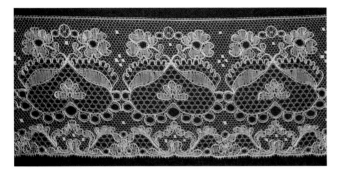

The flowers and open circles are typical Tønder features. Courtesy Bobbi Donnelly.

Blonde

Blonde is named from the creamy colour of the untreated silk usually used to make this lace. The background is a fine point ground (occasionally kat stitch) and the motifs are usually large-scale flowers and leaves, worked in cloth stitch with glossy silk floss and thick outlines. Blondes were first made in the 1750s, becoming highly fashionable around 1815 and continuing to be popular to the end of the nineteenth century. Advances in the preparation of silk led to a stronger thread that could be dyed or bleached, leading to the making of black Blondes and white Blondes. The main centres of production were Chantilly, Caen and Bayeux.

Chantilly

This is a lace that was nearly always worked in a matt black silk known as grenadine. The lace developed in the same centres as Blonde when black lace became fashionable in the 1840s. Very large black shawls were made in the 1860s. The ground may be point ground or kat stitch, and the motifs are worked in half stitch, or part half stitch and part cloth stitch, giving a relatively light effect. Honeycomb stitch is used as a filling and there are strong outline gimps, which are usually composed of bundles of threads. Large items are made up of strips joined with a special stitch known as Point de Raccroc. This stitch is

The fine silk threads of Blonde lace grounds are very fragile, so it is not unusual to find surviving examples in this state. The cloth-stitch areas, worked with thick floss silk, tend to survive better than the point ground. 19cm × 22.5cm.

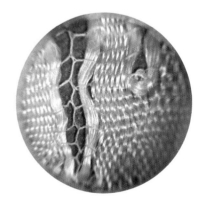

Detail of Blonde showing the closely packed threads of the cloth stitch, and the bundle of threads that form the outline gimp.

nearly invisible when first made, but it is a weak part of the lace and splits may occur along the joining line. If there is no sign of a join in a large item of Chantilly it is probably machine made, so look for other signs such as a picot edging that has been stitched in place or gimps that have cut ends at both start and finish of a motif. (See Machine Lace in Chapter 9.)

Bonnet veil of Chantilly lace – we searched but could find no sign of a join so it seems that this veil was worked in one piece. It would have required an extremely large pillow, hundreds of bobbins and a very skilled lacemaker. Maximum width 88cm, depth 39cm.

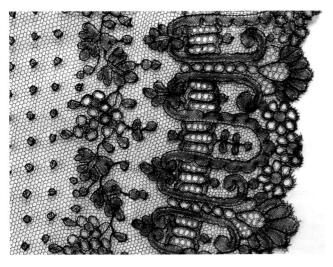

The detailed image shows the fine thread forming the slightly irregular hexagonal mesh. Leaves and other features are half stitch, honeycomb rings give the open spaces and there are thicker outline gimps around all the main features. Clearly visible on the right of each of the dots are the little ends showing where the gimp threads were cut (if it was machine made there would be cut ends on both sides).

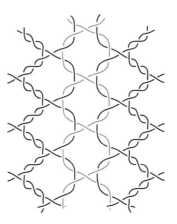

Diagram showing the Point de Raccroc stitch (grey line) used to join two widths of point ground. The use of this stitch meant large pieces of lace could be made by several workers, allowing a more rapid response to changes in fashion demands.

Lace with Other Mesh Grounds

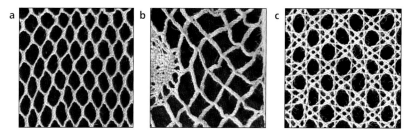

a. Mechlin ground, also called *eis* ground: this is a hexagonal mesh with twisted pairs on four sides and short plaits on the verticals.
b. Valenciennes, known as square or diamond ground: it usually appears as a diamond mesh with plaits on all four sides, often worked without pins giving an irregular finish. **c**. Flanders ground: a mesh of squares worked with groups of four pairs.

Mechlin

Mechlin (also known as Malines) was one of the delicate laces made in Flanders during the eighteenth century and widely used as a gathered lace. Designs are similar to Valenciennes (right) but always have gimp outlines. The ground was slow and expensive to make and by the beginning of the nineteenth century had been more or less replaced by point ground which is quicker, and therefore cheaper, to work, so it is rare to find a piece of lace with eis ground and you may need magnification to confirm that it is a piece of Mechlin.

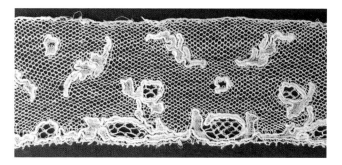

Part of a Mechlin edging with Mechlin *eis* ground surrounding cloth-stitch motifs that have gimp outlines and very simple fillings. The lace appears to have been well used. Probably made at the beginning of the nineteenth century when Mechlin was going out of favour.

Valenciennes

Valenciennes is a net-based lace that, like Mechlin, became fashionable in the eighteenth century. In contrast to the point-ground laces, Valenciennes never has an outline gimp, so the lace is completely flat. Initially a variety of grounds were used, but by the start of the nineteenth century most Valenciennes was made with the diamond mesh that has a plait along each of the four sides. Enormous quantities of Valenciennes edgings and insertions were produced throughout the nineteenth century, mainly for trimming underwear and baby clothes. The absence of a gimp means it is an easy lace to copy by machine, and machine and handmade versions seem to have been equally valued and may even appear on the same garment.

A Valenciennes edging (2cm wide) with diamond ground, cloth-stitch circles and shallow headside scallops. The irregular picots on the headside, each formed by a twisted pair, also show that this is hand not machine made.

Flanders

A great variety of needle and bobbin lace has been made in Flanders (Belgium) since the sixteenth century, but the lace described as Flanders lace is a nineteenth-century bobbin lace with square-mesh Flanders ground being a distinctive feature. Motifs within the ground are usually outlined with a pair of threads, and often have a thicker gimp thread within that outline.

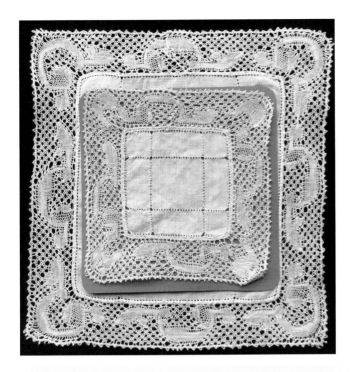

In Flanders this is known as the *aape* (monkey) pattern. The two mats were acquired together but the designs are not identical. Typical features are the square Flanders ground and worked (not gathered) corners. Outlining pairs are visible around the motifs, but there are no gimps so the lace would have been quicker to work than a lace where thicker threads needed to be put in and taken out for every motif. Side of large mat 18cm, small 11cm.

WORKING LENGTHS AND CORNERS

Bobbin lace edgings and insertions made for sale were usually worked as continuous lengths: once the lace was started the lacemaker kept working on the same pattern, sometimes for years. At intervals there was a 'cut off day' when a dealer would call, measure and cut off the completed lace, pay the lacemaker and provide her with new thread. When used for handkerchiefs, mats and so on, lace made in this way needs to be gathered for the corners.

Flanders lace was one of the first everyday laces to introduce worked corners. The technique here is to have a pricked pattern for a square of edging; the lacemaker would then work round and round, removing pins at the start so the pattern could be re-used and long lengths with corners were worked as continuous spirals. To finish a square, the start is placed over a matching section of the fourth side and firmly stitched in place; excess lace is then cut off from front and back of the lace along the stitching lines. The process is repeated with the cut edge being the start of the next square. This method of finishing with an overlap means that in a set of mats the joins will be in different positions along the sides. Unfortunately, with lace made for the mass market the join is often badly made, bulky and likely to come undone (*see* illustration above). With the same type of finish in a top-quality piece the join is barely visible.

Corners for other laces such as Torchon and later Bucks Point were designed in the twentieth century, mainly for the amateur market. These usually require each piece to be started with bobbins wound in pairs and finished by linking start to finish while the lace is still on the pillow – a much slower, and therefore more expensive, process.

Corner of a 4.5cm wide border designed by Ulrike Bohm and worked by Diana Blackburn. The background is Flanders ground, there are picots along the headside and the rest of the features including the pea motifs are cloth stitch. On the left there is an area of slightly denser ground where the two ends of the border have been carefully joined.

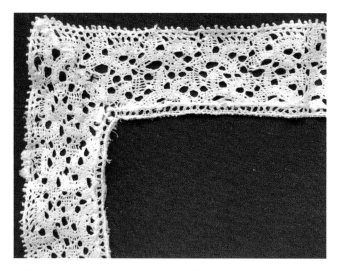

This example of a nineteenth-century Binche edging does not really have a ground, but the beginnings of peas and snowflakes are visible in the rather amorphous design. 3cm wide.

Binche

Eighteenth-century Binche was a densely patterned lace worked with a fine thread and often including tiny round motifs, which in later Binche laces were described as snowflake or pea grounds. Twentieth-century Binche is closely related to Flanders but with a much greater variety of grounds. From the 1960s onwards there has been a great interest in Binche lace, with lace schools in Bruges attracting students from all over the world to design and work complex lace, often pictorial, for the joy of the challenge.

Ipswich lace

During the second half of the eighteenth century there was a thriving lace industry in the town of Ipswich in Massachusetts, USA. Samples of the Ipswich lace, made between 1789 and 1790, have been preserved in the Library of Congress. These are all edgings worked in black silk. Many have the appearance of Bucks Point, but the grounds are either kat stitch or Torchon. It is known that linen laces were also made in the town and the industry continued until the 1820s when machine lace began to take over.

It is unlikely that Ipswich laces will turn up in Britain but they are worth looking out for in the US.

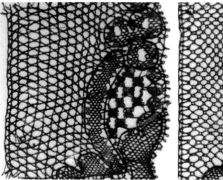
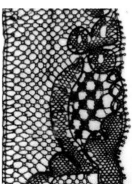

Two examples of Ipswich lace. The one on the left has kat stitch ground, on the right the ground is more like Torchon ground, but not worked at 45 degrees. The same cloth-stitch motif, with gimps and filling of small blocks appears in both laces (6.5cm and 5cm wide). Courtesy Karen Thompson.

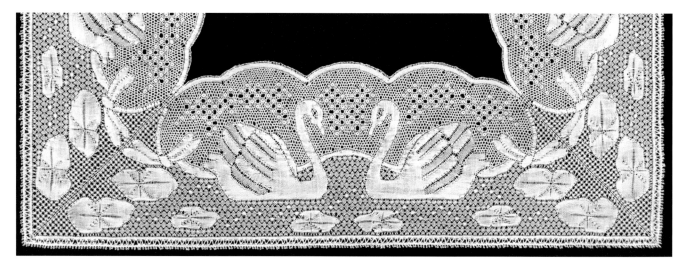

Border (9cm wide) of twentieth-century Binche lace with swans and lily pads, designed by Grace Jones and worked by Diana Blackburn. This border includes a much greater variety of stitches and textures than the Flanders ducks border. Some of the swans' feathers are half stitch, the main background of the sky is kat stitch with clouds of snowflakes, while the water is a more formal arrangement of larger snowflakes and pea motifs.

Metal thread lace

Some of the earliest bobbin lace was made with metal thread (usually composed of a flattened silver-gilt wire twisted round a silk core). A little of this lace has survived, mainly on items such as gloves, but much has been melted down for its bullion content. Metal lace is still made in Germany, and to a lesser extent in other countries, but without any provenance it is difficult to date any examples you find, or say with any certainty where the lace was made.

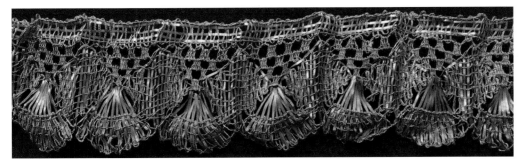

This length of metal lace has two types of thread, one flat, one rounded. It is pleated in a way that is often used on Norwegian traditional costume, but this does not necessarily mean that it was made in Norway. 5cm wide.

Metal lace of this type has been widely used on clothing and also in churches and synagogues. There are glimpses of the original gold colour, but most of the thread has tarnished to a dark brown, which is not unusual with old metallic lace. 3.5cm wide.

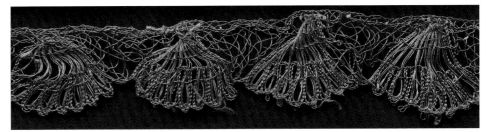

Freehand lace

Freehand lace can look very like Torchon, but the working method is different and this shows up as subtle differences in the finished lace. Freehand lace is worked without a pattern and pins are only placed at the outside edges, which means there are no pinholes visible within the stitches (as they may be in Torchon). Another difference is that the way tension is applied means that the angle of the ground is rarely 45 degrees. Freehand lace is still widely made in Scandinavia, Alpine regions, and Russia.

Length of Mikhailov lace, a Russian freehand lace bought by Gil's grandfather while serving there during the First World War. The angle of the ground is less than 40 degrees and there are no holes in the centre of the stitches, which indicates that it has been worked freehand. 3cm wide, 4cm repeat.

A photo of freehand lace being made in Sweden in 2000. Note the striped fabric, which acts as a guide for placing the pins at each side and keeping the lace straight. No pins are used in the central area so careful tensioning is needed to form the cloth-stitch motifs.

Five examples of guipure bobbin laces; three are edgings, one is an insertion and the fifth is a galloon intended for surface decoration.

CHAPTER 4

CONTINUOUS BOBBIN LACE WITH PLAITED GROUNDS

Laces without a mesh background are often described as guipure laces. Bobbin lace guipures include Genoese, Maltese and Bedfordshire, together with a variety of other laces such as those known as Cluny and Le Puy. In reality there are rarely clear distinctions between these bobbin lace guipures, but some of the styles with distinctive features are described here as separate laces.

Guipure laces were made in the sixteenth and early seventeenth century before the grounded laces developed. They are composed mainly of plaits, picots and twisted pairs, with other features such as tallies and small areas of cloth stitch gradually coming into the designs. Many early laces of this type are recorded as Genoese, although the lace was made across Italy and in many other parts of Europe including Flanders and Britain. The style of lace remained popular in peasant communities and was widely copied at the end of the nineteenth century, while in a few regions, such as Bedfordshire in England, the guipure laces began to include large areas of cloth stitch for flowers and foliage set within a background grid of plaits with picots.

Genoese

As lace evolved in the sixteenth century much of the linen bobbin lace was worked in imitation of the slightly earlier needle lace known as cutwork or reticella. Initially known as 'bone lace' or 'bone work', this style of lace acquired the name Genoese, from the city where much was made. These laces were widely used alongside needle-made laces for the elaborate ruffs and cuffs we see on sixteenth- and early seventeenth-century portraits.

The likelihood of finding early Genoese lace is small, but several late nineteenth-century lace industries specialized in reproductions of old laces, which were often very good copies of the early lace.

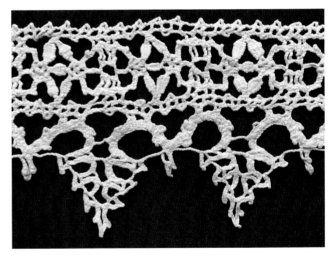

This combination of insertion and 'fir-tree' scallops can be found in many collections around the world including England, America, Switzerland and Australia. Some may be original seventeenth-century laces, others are known to be reproductions from around 1900; most are about 7cm wide. This example, a gift from Alan and Vanessa Hopkins, is probably from the Winslow lace industry in England, which in 1908 was advertising: 'Reproductions of Antique Pillow Laces'.

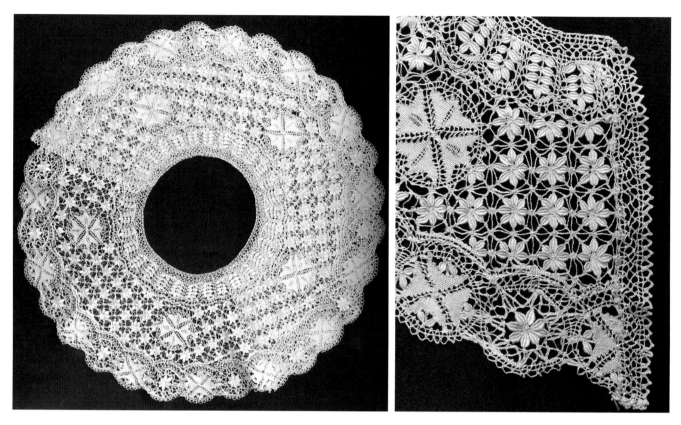

A high-quality Maltese collar dating from around1860. Like many examples of Maltese lace from that time, this collar is large: 15cm wide and 230cm along the outside edge, so placed flat it forms more than a circle and a half. A collar of this type was known as a bertha and worn around the shoulders of a low-cut dress. Details of the construction can be seen in this end section of the collar (right). The main part is three distinct bands (probably by three different lacemakers) linked along their edges. A separate edging has been stitched across the ends. The middle section is mainly rosettes each composed of eight fat tallies; spaced along this panel are eight Maltese crosses each in a ring of twisted pairs. The outer edge has simpler crosses, alternating with rings containing single rosettes; the cuts across the ends suggest this section was worked as a straight strip which had lengths cut off as required. The neck edge has a row of leaf sprays each with nine leaf-shaped tallies and the tightness of the neck edge indicates this was worked on a curved pattern.

Maltese

Maltese lace is a direct descendant of Genoese lace. In 1830 lacemakers from Genoa were brought to the island of Malta to improve the skills of local women. Initially the style was much the same as the seventeenth-century Genoese laces, but the lace was worked in silk not linen and developed a distinctive style. By the 1850s Maltese lace, made from rich creamy-gold silk, had become highly fashionable and it was very well received when exhibited at the 1851 Great Exhibition in London. About that time the Maltese Cross was introduced into every Maltese pattern – an early example of branding – which makes this lace easy to identify. Maltese lace is usually made up into large items such as collars and shawls, each composed of two or more strips of lace loosely

stitched together along the sides. The stitching line can usually be seen (and is often coming apart as in the example below). The best Maltese lace was worked in cream or black silk; later examples, worked in cotton, are rarely of the same high quality.

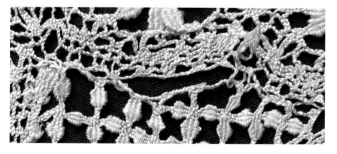

Broken line of stitching in a Maltese collar.

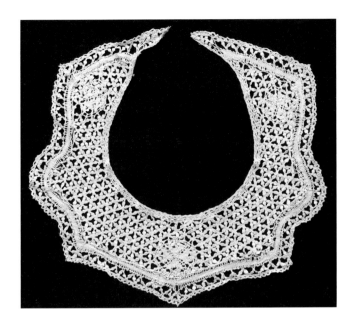

A Maltese collar of a very different quality, brought back from Malta by a soldier stationed on the island during World War I. It was probably bought from a box of locally made lace taken into a hospital for wounded servicemen to buy souvenirs.

Bedfordshire

Lace designers from the English East Midlands were strongly influenced by the Maltese lace seen at the Great Exhibition in 1851, and over the following years the lace made in Bedfordshire, Buckinghamshire and Northamptonshire gradually changed from mesh grounds to guipure. For many years these guipure laces were called Bedfordshire Maltese, but they are now usually described as Bedfordshire.

There were two reasons for the popularity of guipures. The first was fashion: this type of strongly patterned lace looked much better than delicate net-based laces on the strong colours and bold outlines of tailored jackets and spreading crinolines. The other factor was that guipure laces could not initially be copied by machine, so lacemakers who were able to switch to the heavier laces could, for a few years at least, continue to earn a living from their craft.

By the 1870s machines were making effective copies of guipure laces and the hand workers could no longer compete. Their industry might have survived with its reputation intact if it had then concentrated on the high end of the market. Instead lacemakers worked at speed, taking less and less care in their work, often using poorly designed or worn out patterns so the lace was badly made and barely worth the effort of attaching to a garment or table linen. By the end of

the century few lacemakers had the skills to work the more complex designs so little advantage could be taken of the Art Nouveau and Arts and Crafts movements. Unfortunately, a lot of the bad lace survived and it is this lace that was remembered when attempts were made to rescue the craft in the twentieth century.

Bedfordshire lace works well for items such as collars with large floral designs. Many pattern drafts for wider edgings and collars were signed by the designer, with John Sergeant and Thomas Lester being the best known. In the 1870s Lester specialized in large pieces for caps, collars and lappets. Most of Lester's designs were flowers and foliage, but a few featured animals and exotic birds such as eagles and ostriches. Many of the complex patterns could only be worked by the most experienced lacemakers who were able to interpret a new design, often making it just once for an exhibition or special commission. For secrecy these pieces might be worked in the designer/dealer's workshop while most Bedfordshire lacemakers were working in their own homes.

A trio of Bedfordshire edgings, all with the plait and picot headside known as 'nine-pin'. The footsides are all different with the middle one being most commonly found. Plaits with picots form the background of all three laces and all have a wavy cloth-stitch trail, the first and third include tallies. The lower example has some unusual features for an edging including spaces within the trail, an open footside and tallies that are worked over cloth stitch. It is quite possible that this is a lace that has come from a different lace tradition. 4.5cm, 3.25cm and 5cm wide.

This collar, made in the second half of the nineteenth century, has the same plait and picot headside seen on the narrower Bedfordshire laces, while the internal area features naturalistic leaves and flowers worked mainly in cloth stitch. Most of the lacemakers who were working Bedfordshire lace in the second half of the nineteenth century had previously made Bucks Point, so it is not surprising to find small areas of point ground in the centre of the flowers. Other ground stitches taken from Bucks and Honiton can be found as fillings and grounds in Bedfordshire designs.

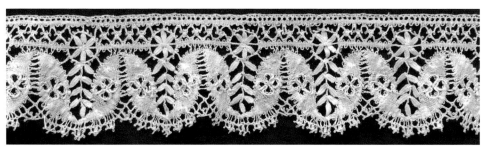

An example of a high-quality Bedfordshire edging with well-formed tallies, plaits with picots and the advanced technique of gimps around internal features. The headside has a complex arrangement of plaits with picots. 4.5cm wide, 3.5cm repeat.

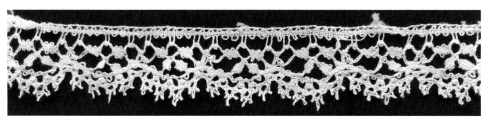

In contrast this is a poor-quality Bedfordshire edging. It does have a plait and picot headside, but the tallies are irregular and the lace was obviously worked at speed, and probably on a well-worn pattern that could not support the pins. 2.5cm wide.

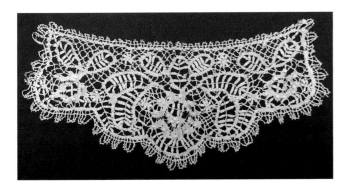

Leaf shapes and rather scrappy flowers are visible in this cuff, which was probably made towards the end of the nineteenth century. The leaves are simple in structure with long tallies indicating the veins – at an earlier date it is likely that the leaves would have been cloth stitch, more like those in the collar opposite. There is a wide plait-and-picot edging to the headside, and a smaller one along the footside, which indicates the cuff was intended to be attached to the surface of a sleeve.

Probably originating towards the end of the nineteenth century, the pricking for this lace was found in a Northampton junk shop and has been used extensively over the past forty years by amateur lacemakers to practise the more advanced Bedfordshire techniques. The all-round footside suggests that the panel was intended as an insertion, but it works equally well as surface decoration.

Cluny and Le Puy

There is a long history of lacemaking in and around the French city of Le Puy. The industry had declined by the end of the eighteenth century, but there was a revival in the 1830s when Le Puy became known for its black silk guipures. White guipures, made later in linen, are usually described as Cluny.

Today if you search online for 'Cluny lace' you are likely to find lace made on a Leavers machine. This type of Cluny lace was first made in Nottingham (England) 150 years ago and there is still a Cluny lace company on the Nottinghamshire/Derbyshire border, but most Cluny lace is now produced in China.

The original Cluny lace was a French guipure bobbin lace, which acquired its name in the second half of the nineteenth century. The name was probably coined as a marketing ploy when sales of lace made in Le Puy were beginning to decline. Although there is no record of a lace industry in the town of Cluny the lace merchants in Le Puy were able to increase sales by linking the name with an important collection of lace in the Cluny Museum, established in Paris in the building that had once been the town house of the Abbots of the Cluny monastery.

A length of black silk edging, probably Le Puy, featuring a version of the motif known in Britain as the 'paisley pear', which was widely used on other textiles, especially shawls, but is relatively rare in bobbin lace. The structure of the headside is unusual and many of the bars that appear to be plaits are actually very slim tallies. 9cm wide, 5cm repeat.

Two more examples of black guipure bobbin laces (7.5 and 10cm wide) probably from Le Puy. The motifs and grounds are more geometric than those we would see in Bedfordshire guipures.

A Cluny insertion composed of plaits, twisted pairs and long, thin tallies. 3.5 wide, 8cm repeat. This insertion matches an edging shown in an early twentieth-century sample book produced by the Cheefoo industry in China.

Cluny doily, a small one (14.5cm in diameter) from a set of different sizes. This is also likely to have been produced in China, but could have been made in almost any lace-making district in the early years of the twentieth century. Quality of workmanship is good with well-shaped tallies and good overall shape (indicating an accurate pattern).

A butterfly or moth motif with the body worked as two long tallies occurs frequently in Cluny laces. Here a 3cm wide edging has the tallies over half-stitch wings. The lace has been gathered to go round the corners of a small table cloth. Courtesy Veronica Merryweather.

Fleuri de Craponne

Flowers with five or more petals worked in half stitch and surrounded with a gimp are typical for this lace named after Craponne, a small town about 25 miles (40km) from Le Puy. In the nineteenth century the lace from Craponne was highly regarded for its beauty and richness, and found a ready market in the local cities of Lyon and Saint-Etienne.

Insertion and border of black yak lace featuring plaits and picots, wheel motifs crossed by square-ended tallies (wheat-ears), and a scalloped headside on the border. 3.5cm and 6.6cm wide.

Corner of a handkerchief bought at a market in Paris in 1992, edged with Fleuri de Craponne lace.

Yak Lace

Yak lace, also called worsted lace, is a Victorian guipure lace. The thread is usually black worsted (long-staple wool), but white, cream and even coloured examples are found. Patterns are mainly Cluny or Bedfordshire in style, but there are examples that are more like Torchon. Yak was mainly used for trimming the heavy daytime fashions of the day, but was also used for furnishings.

Fashion plate from an 1876 edition of *The Ladies' Treasury* showing how yak lace might be used. The caption reads 'Dolman Mantle with long ends in front, made of black cashmere and trimmed with gold braid, open work, worsted lace insertions and lace.'

New and revived bobbin lace industries

At the end of the nineteenth century the handmade lace industry in England was in a poor way with many lacemakers struggling. There was still a demand for 'real lace' for clothing and household items, but no system for getting new patterns and thread to the lacemakers, nor lace to the buyers. Efforts to improve the situation were made by a number of individuals and groups who managed to establish local industries, such as the Bucks Cottage Workers' Association and the Winslow Lace Industry, using the surviving small pool of lace skills.

Missionaries and philanthropists also introduced lace to various parts of the world to provide occupation and income for women and girls (and occasionally men). Records from the nineteenth and early twentieth centuries show lace being made in India, Ceylon, Malaya, China, Brazil, St Helena, Japan, North America and South Africa. A few remnants of these industries have survived, notably on the island of Sri Lanka. In all these areas lace was made for sale to visitors and temporary residents who took it home as mementos or gifts. Some of this lace has inevitably remained in family collections, so knowing the family history may help to identify and date the lace.

Sri Lankan lace

We are finishing the chapter on continuous bobbin laces with a group of laces from Sri Lanka, an island that has a long history of making lace for the local and tourist markets. The examples show a variety of bobbin laces that can be dated with a fair degree of accuracy, but are not necessarily easy to identify as any named lace style. Some were acquired by tourists in Sri Lanka (formerly known as Ceylon) between 1969 and 2004.

At the end of 2004 the coastal area of Sri Lanka, where most lacemakers worked, was devastated by a tsunami. One of the organizations set up to support the recovery programme was the Power of Hands Foundation. This group encouraged lacemakers to move away from doilies and produce items that were more likely to be attractive to the tourists who were gradually return-ing to the island. They also made contact with a film company in England which commissioned lace for period dramas such as *Jane Eyre*. In 2008, a group from the Foundation travelled to England to promote the work of the Sri Lankan lacemakers and sell their lace through textile fairs and other events.

These doilies are a traditional Ceylonese design known as an elephant's foot. The largest (21cm in diameter) was bought by Adrienne Thunder during a visit to the island in 2004. The other two are nearly seventy years older, bought in 1936 by Vivien Boulton's father for his bride-to-be when he returned from Ceylon where he had been working as a salesman for Twyfords. The older doilies are smaller, and the little one (12cm) much simpler in design, but the two larger ones are remarkably similar.

Two edgings bought by Jean's mother in 1969, each 1.5cm wide. The lower length is a style of lace we have not seen elsewhere, the upper one can be described as Cluny.

Two small mats (9cm and 12cm sides) the upper one was bought by Adrienne on her visit in 2004, the lower one was bought by Gil's sister in 1991 when she was told the design was Jasmine and the tourist information said it was Brussels lace – we would call it Torchon.

Bracelet (9cm) bought from the Power of Hands Foundation (note the similarity of this pattern to the Cluny butterfly edging on an earlier page).

Heart motif (7cm across) bought at the Knitting and Stitching Show in London in 2008.

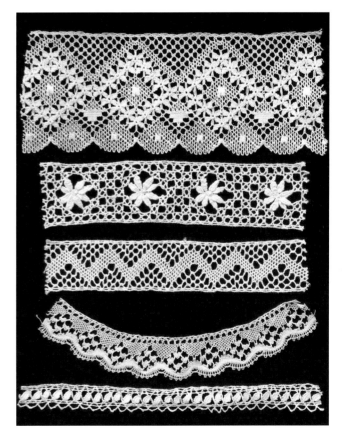

These samples were given to Lilian McCormick when she visited a fashion/textile college in Galle, in 2012. The college supported both the makers of handmade lace and a thriving fashion industry in Sri Lanka, which demanded more lace than could be supplied by the local lacemakers. That explains the mix of machine and handmade lace in this group: the laces at top and bottom of the picture are machine made, the other three are locally made bobbin laces. All the laces, which range in width from 1.5cm to 7.5cm, are examples of lace the college was using for clothing or domestic linens.

Early nineteenth-century flounce of Brussels bobbin lace.

CHAPTER 5

NON-CONTINUOUS BOBBIN LACE

Non-continuous bobbin laces can be divided into two main groups: pieced laces where motifs are made separately and then joined, and braid laces, where a braid, worked with relatively few pairs, meanders across the pattern with links (sewings) where parts of the braid touch. In both pieced and braid laces any spaces between the main features may be left open, crossed by twisted or plaited bars (with or without picots) or filled with ground stitches.

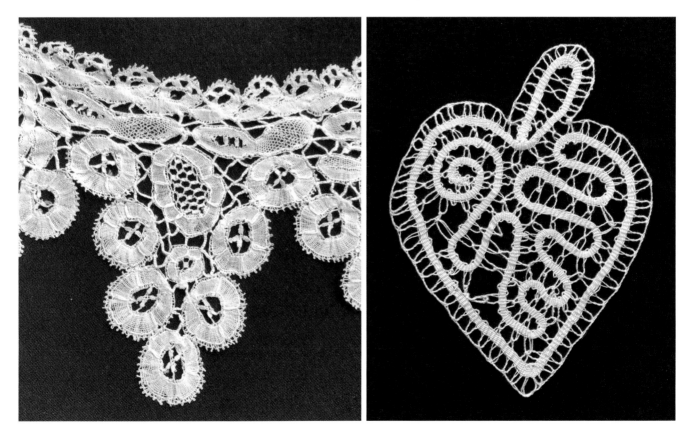

Part of a nineteenth-century collar of pieced lace (on the left) and a twenty-first century braid-lace leaf. The motifs (known as sprigs) of the pieced lace have been worked separately and linked with plaited bars. The single braid in the leaf can be followed as it meanders through the inner area and around the outer edge. In both cases 'sewings' have been used to link adjacent sections.

Pieced Laces

Honiton

Honiton lace is England's only traditional pieced lace. Made not only in the town of Honiton, but also in a large area of Devon and neighbouring counties in south-west England. Starting in the seventeenth century, mainly as a cottage industry, the lace continued to be made for sale until the early 1900s. For many years finished lace was collected in central depots ready for transport to London via stagecoach, Honiton was the main collecting point and gave its name to the lace.

In contrast to other lacemaking areas in England, Devon never lost its traditional lace skills. Devon County Council sponsored lace classes until the 1980s, initially in schools, then in adult education classes. When the County Council withdrew its support, the Devon Lace Teachers took over the role of organizing classes and ensuring skills were passed on.

Honiton and similar laces are worked as individual motifs, known as sprigs. Flowers, leaves, butterflies and so on are made separately then assembled into larger pieces. In the best Honiton laces the motifs are outlined with a raised rib or a tight bundle of threads and a great variety of filling stitches are used. Early Honiton lace often had a net ground, either bobbin- or needle-made. The net was expensive to make and as soon as machine net was available (1810 onwards) it was adopted by Honiton lacemakers as a background for their sprigs. In 1865 Samuel Chick, one of a family of Devon lace dealers, wrote from London to his mother in Honiton requesting suitable cheap sprigs for use in the fashion lace he was planning to sell. Samuel was obviously not aiming for the top end of the market, but some high-quality pieces of Honiton are to be found mounted on machine net.

SEWINGS

A technique known as a 'sewing' is used to link parts of pieced and braid laces as the lace is made. The usual tool for a sewing is a small crochet hook which is used to bring a loop of thread though a pinhole in the edge of a completed section; skilled lacemakers may do the sewing with the tip of a needle. The same technique can be used to add new pairs or join start to finish in other types of bobbin lace.

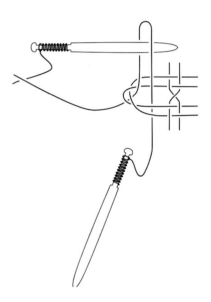

When making a sewing, a pin is removed from where the link is needed, one of the working threads is hooked through the place where the pin had been, the bobbin of the other working thread is passed through the loop and the link is made when the bobbins are pulled apart.

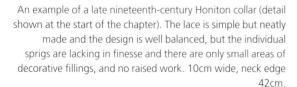

An example of a late nineteenth-century Honiton collar (detail shown at the start of the chapter). The lace is simple but neatly made and the design is well balanced, but the individual sprigs are lacking in finesse and there are only small areas of decorative fillings, and no raised work. 10cm wide, neck edge 42cm.

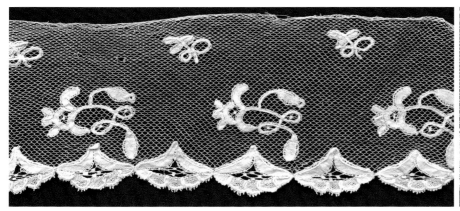
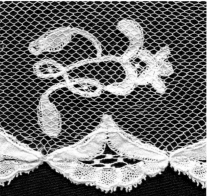

This is an example of Honiton Application, where bobbin-made sprigs are stitched to machine-made net. Three different sprigs are used; two with the narrow braid known as a rib that outlines features in better quality Honiton. The right-hand detail shows the wrong side of the lace where the net has been cut along the edge of a headside motif and can be seen across the back of a sprig. 7cm wide, 6cm repeat.

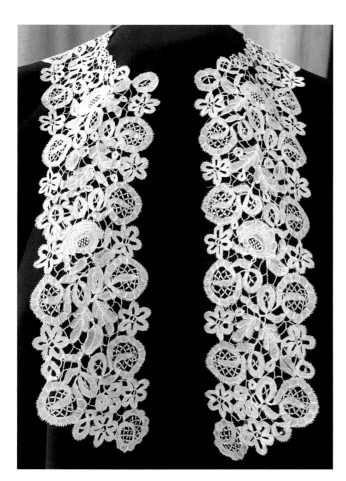

Oval flowers with their two rounds of petals – alternating cloth and half stitch separated by thicker threads – and centres of neat leadworks (tallies) are of rather better quality than other parts of the lace on the left.

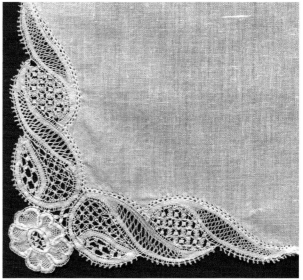

This is a late nineteenth-century Honiton collar, which includes more complex techniques than the previous example. However much of the work is irregular and little care has been given to the overall design. A piece like this would have been assembled from sprigs made by different workers with different skill levels.

This Honiton corner motif is a late twentieth-century sampler, showing a flower with raised outlines and central tallies, curved leaves with a variety of fillings and picots along the outside edge. It is an example of the type of Honiton lace enjoyed by lacemakers from the 1980s onwards, when teaching had spread outside the old Honiton area.

There are thirty or more separate motifs visible in this Brussels lace scallop; the two large motifs in the centre are more or less symmetrical, and the large leaves with side leaflets are almost mirror images of each other, but otherwise the motifs are quite varied. At the lower edge there is a small amount of symmetry but on either side of this there are strongly contrasting shapes.

This scallop is the same basic shape as the previous one, and has many of the same motifs, including the large leaves with side leaflets, but there is one oddity – a leaf with a raised outline and there is a similar leaf in just one of the other scallops. Where did these come from?

It is possible that these odd leaves were inserted later to replace a damaged area, but this seems unlikely as the close-up shows how neatly the leaf fits into the surrounding lace.

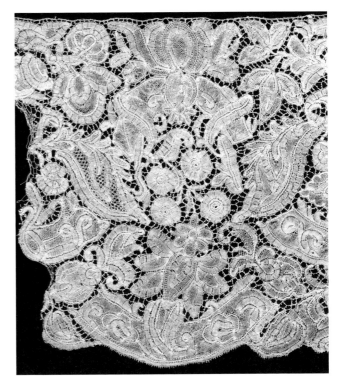

Close to the cut end of the flounce is a large leaf with side leaflets and open ground along the centre. This leaf and one other that has a tiny amount of ground seem to have been worked on the same patterns as those used for the other leaves of this shape.

Brussels lace

The bobbin lace known as Brussels lace was made across Belgium in the eighteenth and early nineteenth centuries. It is a pieced lace usually consisting of large motifs – flowers, leaves and scrolls – worked with a fine thread. Motifs are often formed from a shaped braid that varies along its length. The motifs fit closely together and are linked by plaited bars ornamented with picots. Brussels lace looks impressive, is robust and drapes well, which means it has been popular for wedding dresses and evening wear. One advantage of making pieced lace rather than continuous is that workers can pool their efforts in response to major commissions or changes in fashion.

The illustrations here and at the start of this chapter show small parts of an early nineteenth-century flounce which would once have been gathered above the hem of a skirt. The lace is 31cm wide and would originally have been longer than the current 3.25m (six and a half scallops). Initially there may have been one or more narrow matching flounces, a wide bertha collar and sleeve ruffles. A very large number of lacemakers would have been involved in making this quantity of lace and it is interesting to see the many ways the lace has been interpreted in this one piece. With a detailed study it would probably be possible to identify the work of a number of individuals and their different skill levels.

Every scallop is different, initially they appear symmetrical, but a second look shows this is not the case, similar motifs are repeated in similar positions but the motifs are not identical. Most of the lace is flat, composed mainly of cloth stitch and half stitch but there are two anomalies: two leaves with raised outlines and one with a filling of ground stitches. It would be fascinating to discover how the team who assembled the lace managed to produce such a harmonious whole from such varied elements. The fine linen thread used for the lace gives it a smooth, cool feel and a wonderful drape.

Here are two lengths of early nineteenth-century Brussels lace (each 5.5cm wide) that have been joined to make a 155cm long border which would have given a gently gathered trim (narrow bertha) for a wide off-the-shoulder neckline. Two ends of the lace are shown; on the right the motifs are closely matched, but on the left a variety of different shapes have been used.

Duchesse laces

Brussels lace evolved during the nineteenth century into the type of lace now known as Duchesse lace. Brussels Duchesse and Bruges Duchesse are both composed of mainly floral motifs, usually simpler in construction than the earlier Brussels lace, more widely spaced and linked by plaited bars with picots. Both were made extensively across Belgium, and to a lesser extent in neighbouring countries. The defining differ-

ence between the two types of lace is that Brussels Duchesse includes areas of needle lace while Bruges Duchesse is entirely bobbin lace. An example of a typical Brussels Duchesse collar is shown at the beginning of Chapter 1. Duchesse motifs, like Honiton ones, also work well as an application lace, appliquéd to machine net.

This high-quality Brussels Duchesse cuff (31cm × 5cm) is a mass of flowers and foliage. The central section is a needle-made Point de Gaze panel featuring the small buttonholed rings known as couronnes and there are small areas of Point de Gaze ground. The bobbin lace sprigs – flowers, leaves and scrolls – are detailed with raised veins and outlines. Bobbin-made rings are scattered across the curved leaves and the straight edge.

Neither of these two cuffs has any needle lace and so they are Bruges Duchesse, not Brussels Duchesse. Both were probably made towards the end of the nineteenth century. The first cuff is 28cm long and has a wide machine-made engrelure, which would have tucked inside the edge of the sleeve. The design is simple and the lace has been worked by a skilled lacemaker, but the whole effect has been spoilt by poor-quality thread. The second cuff, part of a set of collar and cuffs, is composed of a variety of motifs including the three-lobed leaves and scroll-ended braids also seen in the narrower collar, plus leaf and flower motifs that can be seen in the Brussels Duchesse laces. 25cm × 7cm.

These flower and leaf motifs form the centrepiece of a large floral spray which is the main design feature of a long stole of Duchesse Application lace (see Frontispiece). The design is beautifully balanced and the motifs are arranged with care on the net foundation. The photo shows the great variety in skill levels required by the lacemakers involved. For example the simplest of braids were needed for the branch of seven leaves on the left, while the complex leaf at the bottom of the picture required a highly skilled lacemaker with good eyesight to manage the raised edges and numerous sewings. The motifs have been invisibly stitched to net, and the net has been cut away from behind the flowers to show the filling stitches. The second image is a close-up of the stole-end showing that in small areas the net has been embroidered, as for Limerick lace, and needle-made couronnes (tiny rings) have been included in the border. It is unusual to find an item such as this beautifully designed piece that is in such good condition and incorporates such a range of lacemaking techniques.

Duchesse lace workshops

Many individuals would have been involved in making a top-quality item of Duchesse lace: the designer who drew out the master pattern; the draughtsman (or woman) who prepared the individual reusable patterns; bobbin lacemakers of different skill levels – some working hundreds of simple flowers, others with greater skills working the more complex motifs including those with raised edges and fillings of different grounds. The Brussels Duchesse lace also needed a different group of lacemakers to produce the needle lace panels. The final stage was assembly. For Brussels and Bruges Duchesse this would be done mainly on a lace pillow with the motifs arranged face down and a lacemaker working plaits, sometimes with picots, to link the sections with sewings, then any needle lace panels were stitched in place. For Application Duchesse an appropriate width of net is stretched over the master pattern, the motifs are arranged right-side up and stitched in place with needle and thread. The lace is finished by carefully cutting away the net from the outside edge and occasionally from behind the larger motifs.

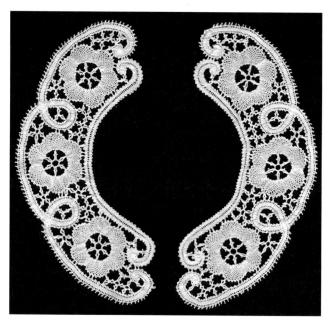

Bruges Duchesse was simplified further in the twentieth century when it became known as Bruges flower lace. This collar shows typical features of the lace: relatively coarse thread, and simple motifs – half-stitch flowers, cloth-stitch braid with scroll ends – with a plait and picot background. Each piece of this collar is approximately 8.5cm wide and 35cm long.

A Dutch version of Duchesse called Withof lace was developed in the 1980s by Sister Judith, from the Withof convent, and her students. The lace is characterized by tightly rolled bundles of threads giving crisp outlines to the motifs. 13cm tall motif designed and worked by Diana Blackburn.

Rosaline lace

Developed in Belgium in the late nineteenth century, Rosaline lace is a part lace where floral motifs and short trails are worked separately and linked by sewings. A common feature is the scattering of needle-made rings (couronnes) across a background of simple bobbin-made motifs. Made commercially in and around the town of Aalet in Belgium from the end of the nineteenth century to 1955.

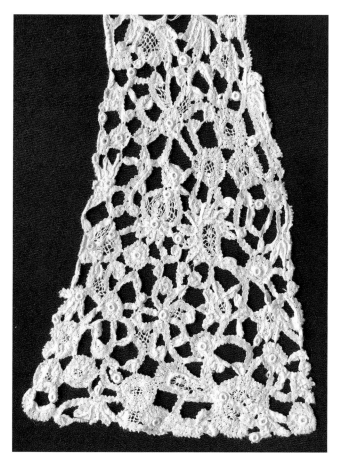

Another Rosaline collar, this one is without couronnes but with far more care given to the overall design, the shaping of the motifs and the linking with picoted bars. This collar is large (13cm wide) and forms a complete circle (51cm in diameter) when laid flat. It was probably made towards the end of the nineteenth century.

End of an early twentieth-century Rosaline collar composed mainly of narrow cloth-stitch braids connecting irregular flowers, some with very simple bobbin lace fillings and most with needle-made couronnes as centres. 13cm across, 80cm long.

Rosaline lace has become a popular lace with Japanese lacemakers. This mat was designed and worked by Japanese lace teacher Chieko Miyawaki in 2003. The main features are the distinctive five-petal roses, each with a central needle-made couronne; the leaf sprays (known as beans) and the petal scallops around the outer edge. The honeycomb filling in the centre is a relatively unusual feature of Rosaline lace (11.5cm × 11.5cm). Courtesy Chieko Miyawaki.

Braid Laces

Bobbin-made braids have been put to use in many ways over the past five centuries including surface decoration, insertions and engrelures (footside edging for other lace). Braids require relatively few bobbins, typically between six and sixteen pairs.

Straight braids are quick and easy to make, and in the past were often made by children and older people whose sight was failing. Braids can also be shaped as they are worked to form a wider lace: the pairs are hung on and worked as a continuous snake that meanders to fill the space required, with links (sewings) where parts of the braid touch. As with the pieced laces, spaces between sections of the braid may be left open, crossed with plaits or twisted pairs, or filled with one of a variety of stitches such as those found in the laces described in Chapter 4. The braid may remain the same or vary along its length. Usually it is possible to trace the path of a single braid throughout the lace, but two or more braids may be present. A variety of named braid laces are illustrated below.

Milanese lace

The braid lace with the longest history is the one we now know as Milanese, although when it first became fashionable in the second half of the seventeenth century it was made in both Flanders and Italy. The lace consists of a meandering

A popular design from Patricia Read's book featuring the braid known as archway. Worked by Sheila Goldsworthy.

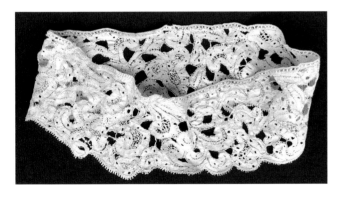

A sleeve ruffle of Milanese lace. No fancy stitches are used, just a simple cloth-stitch braid, gently scalloped along the outside of curves with holes of various sizes in the cloth stitch. A few spaces between the braids are filled with ground stitches, but empty spaces are also an important element of the design. The ruffle has been assembled with an engrelure on one edge and a strip of picots on the other – both machine made. This indicates that the ruffle is nineteenth century (sleeve ruffles were by then relatively unusual); the Milanese lace itself may be much older.

braid, usually varied along the length, which curves and loops back on itself, linked by sewings where parts of the braid touch. The braids are mainly cloth stitch with various arrangements of twisted pairs and changing direction of work, creating a variety of features including rings, waves, spiders and holes of different shapes and sizes. Sometimes the design includes wide gaps between braids; these may be left empty, or filled with simple mesh grounds. Milanese lace was made up into large decorative panels or fashion items such as collars and flounces. It went out of favour in the eighteenth century but has enjoyed a revival in the past forty years, usually in the form of pictorial pieces or small motifs, influenced by Patricia Read's book *Milanese Lace, an Introduction* (published by Batsford in 1988) which introduced many hobby lacemakers to Milanese techniques.

A child's bolero, or dress top, of Russian braid which is composed of two continuous braids that can be traced throughout the internal spaces and around the outer edge. Have you found the ends of the braids? One starts towards the top of the section on the left and finishes at the equivalent point on the right. A shorter braid works the upper part of the back panel. There are numerous sewings. 54cm × 16cm.

Russian braid laces

Russian lace is worked with a simple braid that remains the same throughout, sometimes meandering to leave large spaces that are filled with complex fillings, cleverly worked with just two pairs.

This small mat (14cm across) was bought from the maker in Uglich, Russia in 1998. It is a quickly made piece for the tourist market featuring a simple cloth-stitch braid. The central area of filling, like most fillings in Russian lace, is constructed from a single plait with numerous sewings.

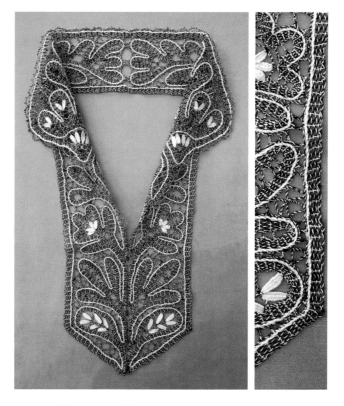

One of the stunning fashion items produced by young Russian lacemaker/designers in the past thirty years. Bought at an international lace congress in 1992. Russian braids often have a line along the middle or edge of the braid composed of thicker threads or a contrast colour, which may appear as a cord or chain. The detail of the Russian collar shows the contrast lines and fillings of leaf-shaped tallies.

Other braid laces

A number of braid laces were developed at the end of the nineteenth century providing lacemakers with techniques that could be learned relatively quickly allowing them to compete with machine-made laces. **Idrija**, from Slovenia, and **Schneeberg**, from Germany, both use six or seven pairs to work tight cloth-stitch braids that open out with the addition of twists. The braids of **Chrysanthemum** lace, which developed in Belgium at about the same time include half stitch and spiders. A completely different style is the twentieth century Spanish lace known as **Hinojosa** worked with a variety of braids

During the last fifty years braids have been widely used for lettering, simple motifs and outlines for more elaborate experimental lace. 5cm tall.

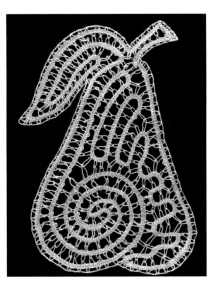

A typical Idrija lace motif composed principally of a tightly worked cloth-stitch braid made with very few pairs, in this case five pairs for the braid that meanders through the inside and a sixth pair with twists that outlines the whole pear. (15cm high) The style was introduced in the 1870s to the lace school in Idrija, Slovenia where it is still made commercially. Worked by Babette Reidy.

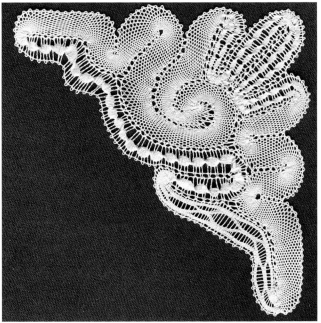

Schneeberg is a quickly worked braid lace that developed in the Erzgebirge area of Germany at the end of the nineteenth century. The very open braid contrasting with narrow cloth-stitch sections is typical of the lace. (9cm tall) Most Schneeberg designs are for motifs rather than larger pieces.

Also known as Spanish witch lace, Hinojosa is a braid lace that was made commercially in the village of Hinojosa de Valle in south-west Spain from around 1920 to 1960, with an amateur revival late in the twentieth century. The lace is worked as a single meandering braid that varies along its length as it fills the whole fabric. Braids use from six to nine pairs and there are just eighteen traditional braids. This example was a gift from Sylvie Nguyen who designed and worked the lace early in the twenty-first century. Four different braids have been used: one braid is mainly half stitch, which is very useful for filling deep curves; two of the braids have a feature that is unique to Hinojosa – a band of cloth stitch twisted at intervals; the fourth braid shows how twists in the worker pair can move a cloth-stitch section across the braid. Longest side 19cm.

Chrysanthemum lace was first made in Belgium (Bruges/Ghent area) in the late nineteenth century, mainly for table linen; today it is more likely to be used for motifs and decorative panels. In this piece, worked by Sylvia Fellows, one side and the end of each of the fingers is cloth stitch and the other side is either half stitch or spiders. In this type of lace, sewings are needed all along the centre line of each finger. 15cm wide.tallies.

In 1924 DMC published a book of patterns and instructions for braid laces intended mainly for household linens (*Les Dentelles aux Fuseaux IIme Séries*). This wide border, with scrolling curves and simple fillings is typical of lace from this book. Relatively unusual for a braid lace is the way the braid crosses over itself. Made in the 1980s; width 11cm.

Cantu lace is in a category of its own. It is not a pieced or braid lace, nor is it a continuous lace although it is worked throughout with the same set of threads. The style of lace was developed in Italy early in the twentieth century and was still being made for sale a century later. This coaster shows the typical Cantu features of hooks, flowers (buds), spurs and linking bars, with picots on some of the bars. 10cm diameter.

Section of the front panel of a Point de Gaze skirt made around 1900.

CHAPTER 6

NEEDLE LACE

Needle lace is a form of detached embroidery that has its origins in the sixteenth century; the main stitch used is buttonhole stitch. Most needle lace is composed of individual motifs linked either by bars or a mesh ground. The exceptions are Hollie Point, made in England from about 1700 to 1810 mainly as insertions for baby clothes, and reticella, widely made in the sixteenth and early seventeenth century with reproductions at the end of the nineteenth.

Hollie Point

Hollie Point is worked entirely in tightly twisted buttonhole stitch with the designs picked out by tiny holes formed by omitting stitches. Designs are usually geometric patterns, but simple flowers and religious texts are also found. Fabric on either side of a Hollie Point panel is always neatly hemmed and often decorated with simple embroidery.

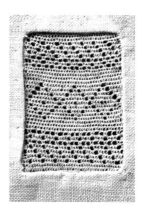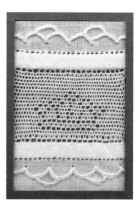

The dense nature of Hollie Point can be seen in these twentieth-century copies. Mini sampler by Karin Jackson, Hollie Point crown by Jean Leader; both pieces slightly larger than actual size.

Needle Lace with Grounds

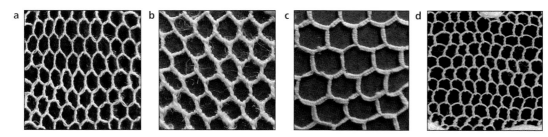

a is Alençon ground, formed by working buttonhole stitch from left to right then whipping back across the tops of the stitches. (If the whipping is tight the mesh may appear rectangular instead of hexagonal – needle lace made in Burano at the end of the nineteenth century often has this rectangular ground.) **b** is tortillé ground where there is whipping along each side of the mesh. **c** is Argentan where each side of the hexagon is closely buttonhole stitched. **d** is the delicate Point de Gaze ground worked with twisted buttonhole stitch from left to right then right to left.

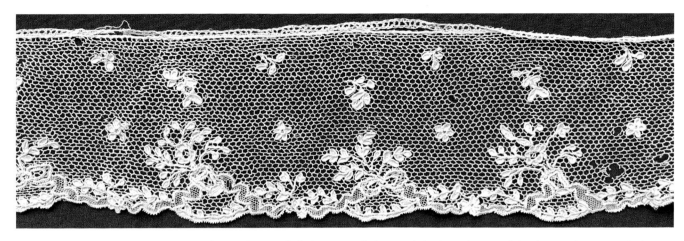

The design of this border with a hexagonal ground is typical of Alençon needle lace made in the early years of the nineteenth century. The larger floral motifs towards the headside are all different but they all include similar ribbons of a closely worked filling. Magnification is needed to show that this filling is Alençon ground while the background mesh is Argentan ground. 6cm wide plus 0.3cm machine-made engrelure.

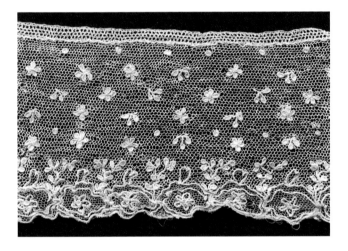

Alençon border with tortillée ground: sides of the mesh are whipped not buttonhole stitched giving a more fragile look than the previous example. Most of the patterning is raised outlines couched to the underlying ground; little dots are buttonholed stitch around individual meshes, enclosed areas contain Alençon ground. 8cm wide plus engrelure.

Needlelace grounds are slow and expensive to make and after 1810 Alençon motifs were often appliquéd to machine-made bobbinet. In this border motifs from a length of Alençon have been removed from the original ground of a wider piece then stitched to machine net with little consideration for the positioning of the motifs, some of which are now cut off or hidden by the machine-made engrelure.

Alençon

Alençon is an example of a needle lace with a mesh ground, which was made extensively in the eighteenth century. Most surviving Alençon is early nineteenth century in the form of borders with a ground of hexagonal mesh and motifs arranged mainly towards the headside. All the motifs have a raised outline formed by working closely packed buttonhole stitch over two or more padding threads. Tiny picots are formed between stitches on the headside. Most of the lace

was produced in workshops, with several lacemakers involved in the making of each piece. This would include girls who couched threads around the outlines of the motifs, some who just made the tiny motifs, others with more skill who could make the larger motifs. Finally, the motifs would go to the lacemaker who made the mesh ground, at the same time connecting the individual pieces. Early nineteenth-century examples of Alençon borders might have tortillé or Argentan ground, but Alençon ground is simpler to work and became more popular when speed was required.

Needle lace motifs, particularly those with a strong but-tonholed outline, are usually robust and survive much better than the bars or mesh that united them, so they can be readily re-used either as individual pieces or assembled into new items. Mrs Treadwin was one of the nineteenth-century dealers who specialized in remodelling old lace into new items such as collars.

Point de Gaze

Point de Gaze is a needle lace that emerged in Belgium in the 1850s. It was shown at the Great Exhibition in 1851 where it was an immediate success. The defining feature is the ground which is a light net, worked in twisted buttonhole stitch from left to right and right to left (giving two twists to the verticals on one row, three on the next). The fineness of the thread and the nature of the stitching produce a gauzy look to the ground, which gives the lace its name.

Other distinctive features include a combination of dense and open stitches – giving a shaded effect – and buttonholed rings (couronnes) that are either dotted across the ground or present as part of a filling. Spaced buttonhole stitches are worked over padding threads around the outlines. Designs are usually floral and from 1870 onwards there are often

Dozens of these tiny needle lace motifs (this one is 3cm across) were found in a bag in a court dressmaker's workroom – they were probably once part of a large piece made in Italy at the end of the seventeenth century. Pretty pieces like this inserted in pendants or brooches can be a relatively inexpensive way of enjoying a small piece of history.

raised petals made separately and stitched in place. The lace has been used extensively for flounces, collars and sleeves (often produced as sets) or even complete garments. For lace with such a fragile ground it is surprising how much has sur-vived, with pieces still being remodelled for wedding dresses.

At the end of the 1860s Point de Gaze had become more flamboyant with large naturalistic flowers and foliage (usually including roses), a greater range of stitches giving a variety of textures, and fillings with open roundels. The magnificent skirt illustrated at the beginning of this chapter, which was acquired by Jean in 2017, shows many of the typical features of Point de Gaze made around 1900.

An example of early Point de Gaze, 1850s or 1860s. A rather formal design with a lot of closely worked buttonhole stitch in the leaves, and flowers with raised veins and outlines. Close buttonhole stitch is the main filling for the motifs, but there are more open areas within the swags and flower centres, and varied textures in the larger leaves and banner shapes. Approximately 9cm wide and each repeat is about 12cm long (not all the repeats are the same length).

HOW JEAN ACQUIRED THE SKIRT

In November 2016, an email came to the Glasgow Lace Group that read:

I have a piece of antique lace in the shape of a very long overskirt. Probably meant to be part of a wedding dress. It has been in my possession for many years wrapped up and would like some advice on what to do with it or to whom to take it for advice.

I invited the owner to bring the skirt to the next group meeting although I was sure it would turn out to be machine made. She arrived with the lace skirt in a plastic shopping bag and as I took it out and looked at it my first thought was, 'It looks like Point de Gaze,' and my second was 'but it can't be – it's a whole skirt!' But looking at it with my magnifying glass confirmed that it was indeed an amazing, wonderful Point de Gaze skirt. And that wasn't all that was in the shopping bag – there was a bodice to go with the skirt, and there were collars too, a small one of Point de Gaze with matching cuffs, a large one of Rosaline bobbin lace, and two large ones both of needle lace. All their owner could tell me about the lace was that it had come from her late husband's family who travelled about a lot, and when I later decided to buy everything for my collection, she was happy to accept my offer.

Sprays of flowers and leaves on the back panel of the skirt. The flowers include roses with extra layers of petals, orchids, lily of the valley and forget-me-nots, among several other plants that are less easy to identify.

Point de Gaze skirt on display at the Glasgow Lace Day (the collars that came with it are on the table to the left). The skirt is 148cm long at the back, graduating to 114 cm at the front, and the design is divided into six sections with a continuous line of little leaves between the sections. The arch of roses above the motif of oval medallions at the lower edge of the skirt spans the whole width of the centre back panel. The medallion motif is repeated with variations, on a slightly reduced scale, five more times around the skirt.

It is rare to find whole garments of Point de Gaze, but small panels are relatively common. This is one of the needle lace sections from the Brussels Duchesse collar shown at the beginning of Chapter 1 (where the rest of the fabric is pieced bobbin lace). The background net is Point de Gaze ground, there are petals and leaves filled with buttonhole stitches and a raised petal also of closely worked buttonhole stitches. Around the needle lace area can be seen the clothwork of the bobbin lace sprigs. Similar needle lace panels are occasionally found in the better quality tape laces or as appliqué on net.

This is the lower part of the front panel of the skirt which manages to combine in a harmonious whole the naturalistic roses, orchids, leaves and other flowers with more formal arrangements of geometric shapes including ovals, scrolls and grids. Also clearly visible are the lines of little leaves that mark out the sections of the skirt. This one section alone includes an amazing variety of stitches and techniques – the oval medallions for example include five different stitch arrangements.

The jacket is quite small and additional pieces would have been needed to complete the outfit. Collars and sleeves are included with similar sets of skirt and jacket in the V&A collection and in the Museum Boymans-van Beuningen in Rotterdam.

This is part of a jacket or bodice that came with the skirt. The floral decoration is so similar to that of the skirt that it seems highly likely that they were intended to be worn together.

Cyprus lace

The name 'Cyprus lace' has been applied to a number of textile techniques. One is needle lace, another is a linen embroidery also known as Lefkara lace (see Chapter 8).

Crochet and Armenian knotted lace, made for the tourist market, may also be marketed as Cyprus lace.

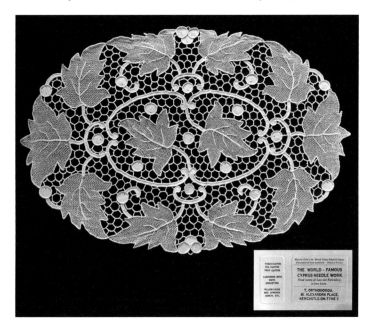

This needle lace mat (45cm × 30cm) from Cyprus is one of the items bought from Mr Orthodoxou who, in the 1950s and 60s, travelled door to door around the north-east of England with a suitcase full of Cyprus needle lace and Lefkara embroidery. Although only simple stitches are used in this piece, it is a well-balanced design with precise workmanship. On his business card Mr Orthodoxou described this lace as 'Point de Venice, made by girls in the British Colony of Cyprus'. Similar lace is made today in China. Courtesy Sheila Priestly.

Irish lace

Many small lace industries were established in Ireland during the nineteenth century, mainly to provide employment for women during the potato famines in the 1840s and 1850s.

Among the needle laces are those made at Youghal, Kenmare and Inishmacsaint. Of these, the most productive industry was the one at Youghal.

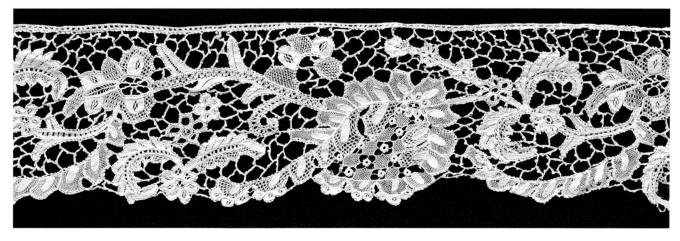

A distinctive feature of Youghal lace is the spaced twisted buttonhole stitch that outlines every motif. Other typical features shown in this border are the floral and leaf motifs within a background grid of plaits with picots, plus a variety of filling stitches giving different textures. 10.5cm wide, 31cm repeat. Courtesy Jo Davies.

Halas lace

This is a type of needle lace that was first made in 1902 in Kiskunhalas, Hungary. The original designs brought together motifs from both Hungarian folk art and contemporary Art Nouveau. It is worked with fine thread, and the pattern motifs are outlined with a thick thread rather than the buttonholed outline found in other needle laces.

This enlarged detail shows the darning stitch that mimics woven fabric and is unique to Halas lace. The thick outlining thread is couched to the design and the needle is taken through rather than around it as the filling is worked.

Halas lace worked with a variety of filling stitches – there are over sixty variations, all worked with a combination of buttonhole stitches. All examples of the lace made in Kiskunhalas contain the trademark three crossed fishes, symbol of the Trinity. These fishes usually fit so well into the design that they are hard to spot – in this piece they make up part of the border. Courtesy Marie Laurie.

Reticella lace

Reticella, a geometric lace with many open spaces, was first made in the sixteenth century when needle lace was evolving from cutwork embroidery (see Ruskin lace in Chapter 8).

The bars and arcs of whipped and buttonhole-stitched threads, and small triangles of closely worked buttonhole stitches in this small reticella coaster (10cm diameter) are typical of pieces made around 1900 in the workshops of the Aemilia Ars Society in Bologna, which specialized in reinterpreting sixteenth- and seventeenth-century lace.

Armenian lace edgings may be worked directly onto the edge of a handkerchief, scarf or other fabric item, or as here, worked over a cord ready for mounting later.

This doily, made in Cyprus, is an example of Armenian lace with a variety of stitch sizes and textures that would have required considerable skill to work.

Armenian lace

This is another form of lace made with a needle, but it has a knotted stitch, which is more closely related to netting (with which it is often confused) than to the buttonholed structure of standard needle lace. This lace has been widely made across the Eastern Mediterranean for edgings and complete items, and has many names including Oya, Bebilla (Bibilla), Smyrna, Palestine and Cyprus lace.

Unnamed Needle Lace

Needle lace is an extremely versatile technique, which requires little in the way of equipment and has been used for hundreds of years for everything from tiny scallops trimming a cuff to full-size garments. Many early needle laces have been copied, and surviving pieces have been remodelled. As a result there are numerous pieces of needle lace that do not fit neatly into any standard classification. One of the laces that evolved in the seventeenth century was the needle lace known as Gros Point, which was popular across Europe for collars, cravats and similar items. The original laces with their multiple layers, variety of stitches and raised outlines decorated with numerous picots, had the appearance of carved ivory. Grinling Gibbons and other carvers were inspired to make copies in wood; usually these were mounted on wooden panels, but there is a story that at least one was worn by its noble owner. Gros Point motifs are robust and often survived into the nineteenth century and were remodelled with new linking bars, to suit the fashions of the day. Copies of the lace were also made.

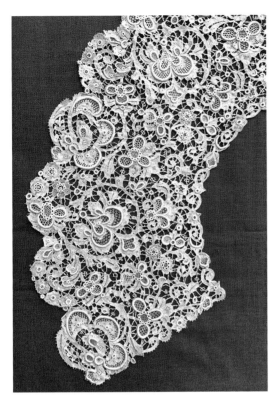

Detail of the collar showing the raised edges to the flowers, neatly worked filling stitches and connecting bars with picots.

This is one end of a large nineteenth-century needle lace collar where the lace is in the style of the seventeenth century. The nineteenth-century copies lack some of the exuberance of earlier lace, but this is an impressive piece of craftsmanship.

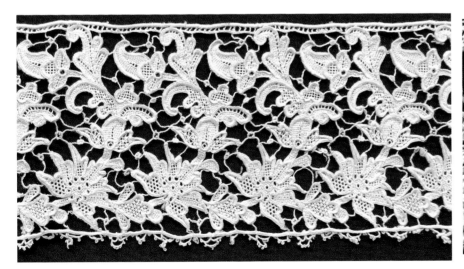

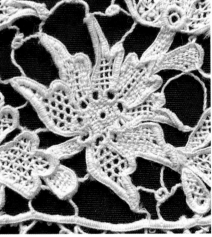

The first impression of this lace is that it is machine made, but the outlines are buttonhole stitch (which machines cannot do), and it is possible to trace needle lace stitching in other parts of the lace. It might be described as Venetian Point (Point de Venise), possibly made early in the twentieth century in Burano, Italy. (9cm wide) Needle lace had been made in Italy from the sixteenth century until the end of the eighteenth, and the industry was revived on Burano in 1870 following a very cold winter which badly damaged the fishing industry (previously the main source of income for the island). The detail shows the buttonhole stitch around the petals and the tightly whipped stitches in the inner area.

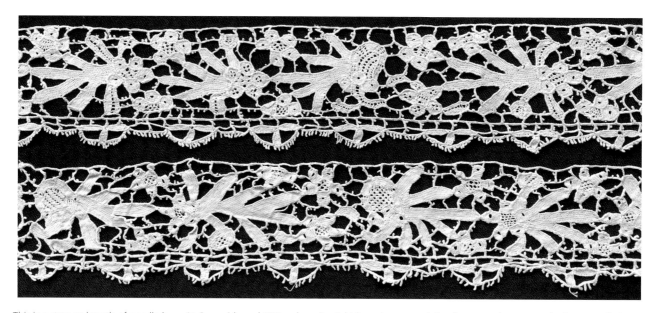

This is a strange length of needle lace. At 6cm wide and 160cm long it might have been an edging for a curtain or even the bottom of a heavy linen petticoat. The main motifs are similar, but are all different and appear to have been worked without a detailed pattern. There are a few raised outlines, but most of the work is completely flat. For the picture the lace has been folded so the top length shows the front of the lace and the lower strip shows the back.

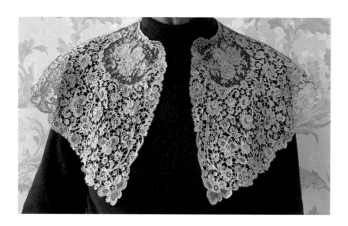

A magnificent collar, which is unusual in that it contains two contrasting styles of needle lace – delicate Point de Gaze panels set in a wide area of much heavier raised needle lace.

Needlelace on a Tape Foundation

The making of needle lace is a relatively slow process, which was speeded up in the nineteenth century by using machine-made tapes to outline design features. Branscombe Point is one of these laces, made first in Devon in the 1860s when the Honiton bobbin lace industry was in decline. The lace is characterized by fine tape, a variety of filling stitches, buttonhole bars with round picots (known as nibs) and an edging of tiny scallops, each composed of five buttonhole stitches.

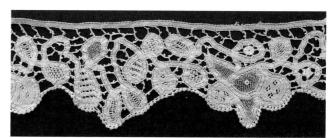

This twentieth-century tape lace is believed to be Branscombe Point. It does not have the delicacy of the early examples that were competing with fine Honiton bobbin lace, but it does have the typical scalloped edge and the distinctive bars with nibs. However the design is poor, the tapes are relatively wide and clumsily shaped and the filling stitches, although varied, are not particularly well worked. (Width 6cm with a 22cm repeat) Contrast this border with the lace in the next illustration.

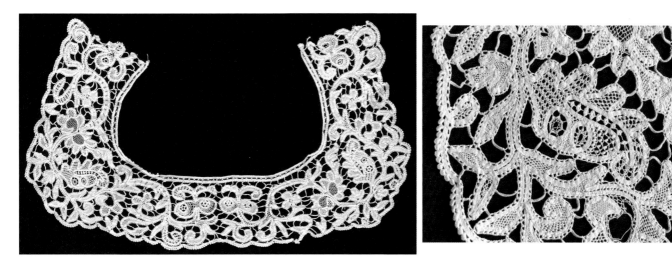

This part of a collar has the look of high-quality Branscombe Point but it lacks the nibs on the connecting bars. That, and the presence of several shamrocks, suggests that the lace was made in Ireland, not Devon, but possibly by someone with a Branscombe connection. 7–9 cm wide. The detail of the collar shows the narrow tapes, tiny scallops on the headside, well thought-out design and a variety of filling stitches that flow with the pattern.

Borris lace is a variety of tape lace that was developed in 1846 by Lady Kavanagh to provide employment for women and girls living on the Borris Estate in Ireland. The lace uses a plain tape, and the best of the early examples included a variety of needle lace stitches. This table mat has open spaces crossed by buttonholed bars, areas filled with a ground of twisted buttonhole stitch, and smaller spaces filled with other needle lace stitches. Courtesy Jo Davis.

In 1906 Lady Kavanagh's granddaughter established a similar lace industry on the Scottish Estate of Ballantrae using the same techniques and patterns as the by then rather simplified Borris lace. This is an example of a doily of Ballantrae lace. (Width of lace 6.5cm.) Note the simple filling stitches, the irregular mesh ground and the machine-made picots around the outside edge. This industry lasted for around twenty years in contrast to the Borris industry, which survived into the 1960s.

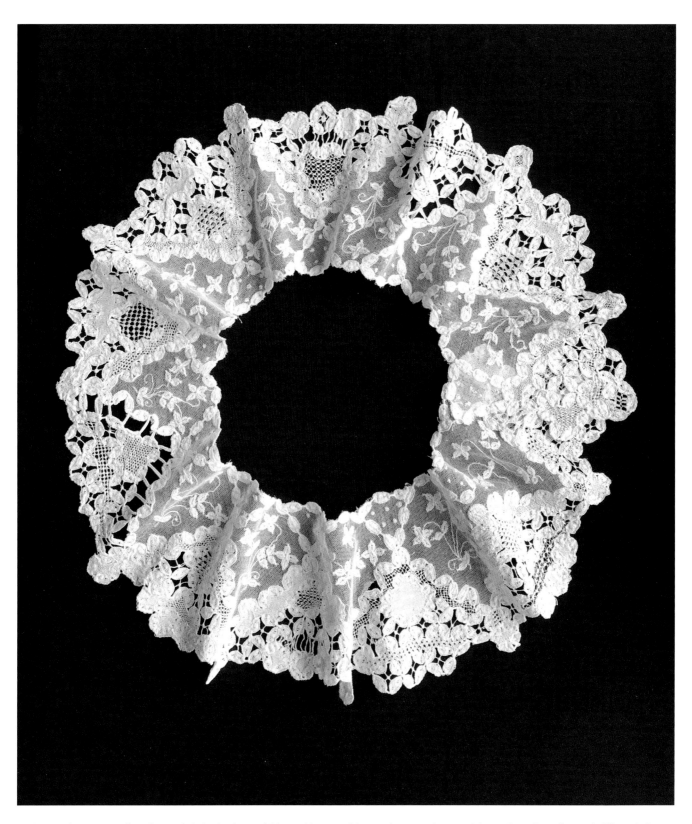

Nineteenth-century collar of Brussels imitation lace, which combines machine-made net and tapes with a variety of needle-made filling stitches.

NET AND TAPE LACES

Net-Based Laces

Using machine-made elements can greatly decrease the time taken to produce a piece of lace that might still be described as 'handmade'. Machine net is found as the background to many varieties of lace, while tapes may provide either structure or detail. Several laces combine machine net and machine tapes with a small amount of hand stitching.

Caufield and Saward recommend that once the tapes have been tacked to the net the embroiderer can use her design skills to choose the stitches for the rest. The lacemaker who produced the collar illustrated at the start of this chapter

has certainly used the opportunity to experiment with her needle lace stitches – there are around forty stitch combinations ranging from closely worked buttonhole stitches to bars and wheels. The background net is exceptionally fine (which would have been expensive) and two sizes of tape of the type known as 'Honiton tape' have been used. Further information about the tapes is given later in this chapter. The collar is 13cm wide and each of twelve repeats is approximately 14cm along the outer edge.

Lace that combines net and tapes is still being made for

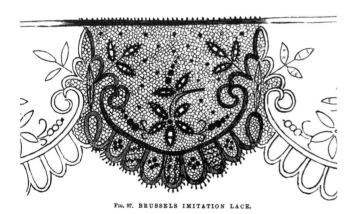

FIG. 97. BRUSSELS IMITATION LACE.

An illustration of Brussels imitation lace (also known as imitation Brussels Point) which is described by Caufield and Saward in their 1882 *Dictionary of Needlework* as 'a dressy lace that washes well, and is the easiest of the imitations to work. It is a net-based lace, usually cream, with simple tapes applied and additional stitching into the net, with a machine-made picot edging.'

A single panel from the collar with the main features outlined by lengths of large Honiton tape, leaves and flowers formed from short lengths of small Honiton tape, six different needlelace filling stitches and small embroidered dots scattered over the net.

The background of this late twentieth-century mat is a net of synthetic thread. The central rosette and the outer border are formed from a scalloped tape, gathered along the straight edge into rosettes; between the rosettes are short lengths of a plain tape decorated with pairs of leaves cut from a different tape; four leaves from the same tape are used in the central motif and there are short lengths of a tiny oval tape forming leaflets on the tendrils. Looking at the back of the work (on the right) it is possible to see how the tendrils are formed from a thick thread that goes in and out of the mesh. The same thick thread has been used for a woven spider and loopy Russian stitch in the spaces between the tapes towards the edge of the lace. A finer thread has been used to stitch the tape to the net. 15.5cm × 11cm.

the tourist market. It may be labelled as 'handmade' and/or 'Brussels', but examples made in the past hundred years are more likely to have been made in China than Belgium, and the hand input is often minimal. Early nets and tapes were cotton; today synthetic materials may be used for either net or tapes. This type of lace is often known as Princess lace.

Machine nets

A machine-made net, known as bobbinet, first became widely available in the second decade of the nineteenth century. Bobbinet has a hexagonal mesh (mimicking point ground) and was initially completely plain, but soon machines were adapted to produce patterned areas, while other machines created mesh of different shapes (see Chapter 9). Some of this net was used as it came from the maker – as dress fabric or veils – but much more was used as the base for a variety of other laces.

In our collections are several bonnet veils, which show a

number of decorative techniques on diamond or hexagonal mesh. The veils are all rectangular with a deep border along one long side, borders (usually narrower) on the two shorter sides and the fourth side slightly gathered. The central area of net may be plain, but more often it is dotted with small motifs (sprigs) which might be put in as the net is made, or applied later by hand or machine. The veils are designed to be attached above the wide brim of a bonnet and dropped down over the face for modesty or to indicate the wearer was not wishing to engage in conversation.

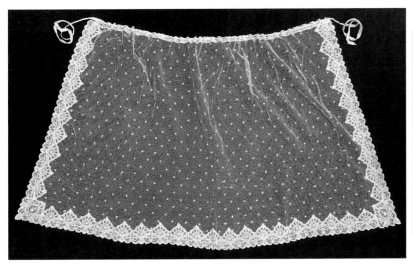

The first impression of a piece like this is that it is an apron, but it is actually a bonnet veil (36cm × 68cm). The background is a plain diamond net, which has been patterned with embroidered dots. Placing these dots so regularly would have been difficult unless their positions were marked beforehand, or the net stretched over a pattern. The borders are also hand embroidered with more elaborate stitching, and the net carefully cut away along the edges. A close-up of the border (right) shows that it is embroidered on a hexagonal net and the back of the work shows where the two types of net have been neatly joined. This seems an unnecessarily complicated way of working, unless it was a case of re-using a border from a damaged item by mounting it on a piece of veiling from another source.

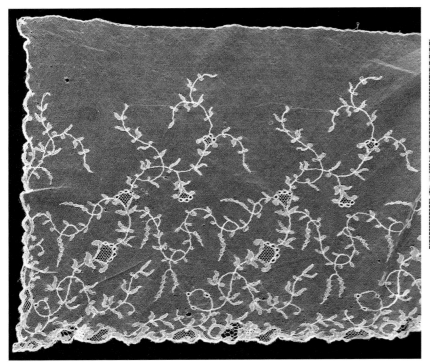

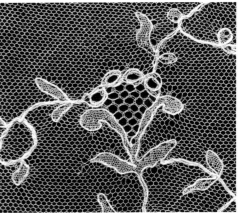

The background of this veil is an example of a patterned net. (40cm × 113cm) It was made on a Pusher machine that could produce small patterned areas in a hexagonal mesh by pulling the threads into a larger mesh (for the flowers) and putting in extra movements (for the leaves). The machine would have been set up specifically for making numerous copies of this veil. A machine-made picot strip has been stitched to the outer edge. The right-hand picture shows the outlines of the tendrils and motifs, which have been run in with a needle and thread. This was a much quicker and therefore less expensive process than working the entire design by hand.

There is more than 250cm of this border, which is 12cm wide but clearly cut from much wider fabric. The background is a fine synthetic net and the decoration is embroidered with white and gold threads. At first it seemed to us unlikely that this amount of embroidery was done by hand, but the image detail on the right shows that the white thread goes in and out of the mesh trapping the gold thread on the surface. As no machine can do this, it must be hand-embroidered.

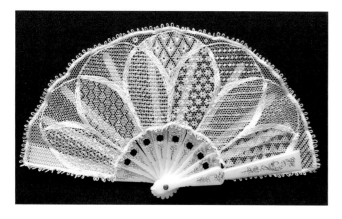

Embroidery on net is often known as Limerick lace (although not always made in Limerick). This small fan leaf shows a dozen examples of embroidery stitches that might be found in a piece of Limerick, in this case worked on hexagonal bobbinet – some of the stitches would look very different if worked on a diamond mesh.

Tambour

Tambouring is a method of working chain stitch on fabric using a small hook. The name comes from the drum-shaped frame (a tambour) on which the fabric was stretched for working in the eighteenth century. Once wide lengths of stable net were available it became the base for tambour lace. In England the main centre was Coggeshall in Essex and the lace is sometimes known as Coggeshall lace. In 1829 Charles Walker, the entrepreneur in charge of the tambour industry, moved with his wife and twenty-four skilled workers to Ireland where they established workshops near the town of Limerick.

The lace made there was mainly tambour. It was worked on cotton net stretched on large rectangular frames, first the chain-stitch outlines, then fillings either worked with the hook in chain stitch, or embroidered with a needle and thread. Limerick is a similar net-based lace but with needle run outlines to the motifs instead of the tamboured ones.

Initially both Coggeshall and Limerick lace were made for the top end of the market, but they came into more general use in the 1840s, at a time when more varied machine lace was becoming available. Lace made for the tourist market towards the end of the nineteenth century often featured shamrocks, roses and harps. Tambour lace has been made in a number of other places including Lier in Belgium and Lunéville in France.

The craft of tambouring had virtually died out by the 1950s, but enjoyed a brief revival in the 1960s and 70s under the guidance of Jean Dudding who introduced coloured threads and other materials in addition to the traditional white on white.

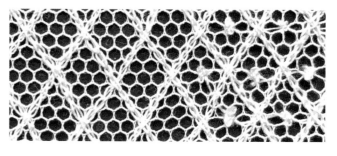

A small piece of tamboured net showing chain-stitch lines and dots.h

A machine was invented in 1865 that could tambour on net, but the slight variations in the patterning of this bonnet veil indicate that it was hand tamboured, including the tiny flower motifs. 35cm × 107cm. The detail of the corner (right) shows the closely worked lines of chain stitch that make up the design.

Tambour with white or coloured thread on black net can be very effective.

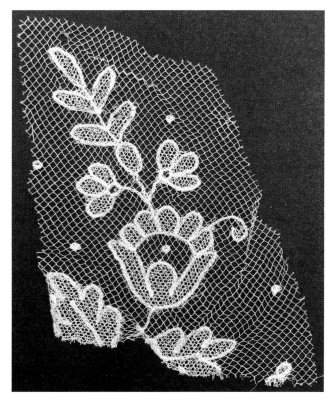

Small sample of tambour worked through hexagonal mesh on top of diamond mesh, with unwanted hexagonal mesh cut away. French or Belgian.

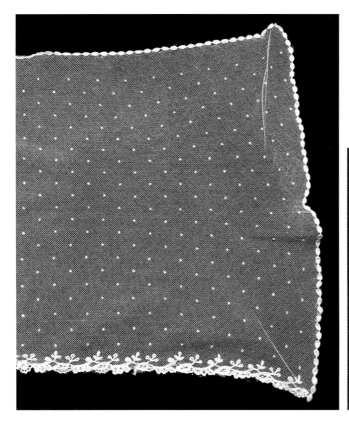

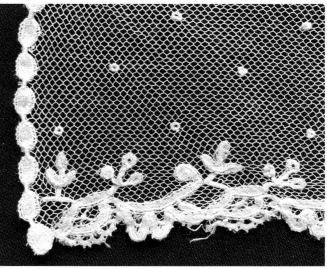

This bonnet veil was sold as Bruges Duchesse, but is actually an application lace. The background is machine-net decorated with tiny hand-embroidered dots. 33cm × 100cm. The detail (right) shows that the lower border is of Honiton sprigs and the side border is a narrow machine-made Honiton tape. Both sprigs and tape are hand stitched to the net.

Application Laces

Machine-made net can also form the background to hand-made bobbin and needle lace, and occasionally tatting or crochet. The net may be the dominant part of the finished lace, or only present in small areas of the background. Handmade lace and machine-made tapes may be present on the same piece.

Honiton tape in various sizes seems to have been one of the most popular of the machine-made tapes, used either as a continuous length or cut into short sections to form leaves, flowers and other small motifs.

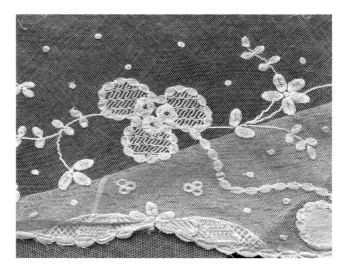

In this battered remnant of a lace collar two sizes of Honiton tape have been used with a few embroidery stitches to form a spray of flowers and a scalloped border. The large flower is about 5cm across.

A small Honiton tape has been used to great effect in this soft fabric collar to form delicate flower sprays and dividing lines between the sections, while a plain tape surrounds the whole collar and areas of embroidered net.

A twentieth-century coaster showing typical Carrickmacross features: strong contrast between fabric and net; thick outline threads; small dots (pops) and loops of thread around the outer edge (twirling). 8cm diameter.

Carrickmacross

Carrickmacross lace is constructed from a layer of fine fabric over a net background. The design is formed by couching a thick thread around the features, with the couching thread going through both fabric and net. The unwanted fabric is then cut away to show the net ground. The net is usually decorated with small embroidered rings known as pops and the whole piece outlined with thread loops known as twirling. The techniques were introduced to Ireland in 1816 by a rector's wife who had collected examples in Italy and taught the skills to women and girls in her village. The village was close to Carrickmacross, but the name was not formally adopted for the lace until 1872. The nature of the construction means that Carrickmacross is not an easy lace to launder, with a risk of the fabric pulling away from the couching and the twirling become untwisted. There is also a horror story of a collector discovering that the dots had been stuck in place, not stitched, so floated away as soon as the lace was lowered into water.

This nineteenth-century collar is an unusually detailed example of Carrickmacross that would have required extreme care and patience in the cutting away of the unwanted fabric. Small, enclosed areas of net have been embroidered and a few areas cut away completely and crossed by bars with picots.

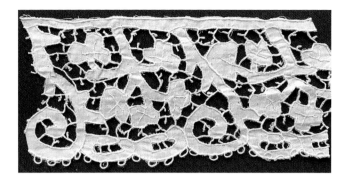

There is also a variety of Carrickmacross known as Carrickmacross Guipure. In this the motifs are outlined with a couched thread and unwanted fabric cut away, but there is no net background, instead the spaces between the motifs are crossed by embroidered bars with picots. The looped twirling edge typical of Carrickmacross is usually present. 5.5cm wide.

Brussels Application is similar to Carrickmacross, but with chain-stitched outlines instead of couched ones. A chain-stitch embroidery machine – the Bonnaz – invented in 1865 was small enough to be used in a home workshop and was often used to work the outlines. In this piece all the stitching is machine chain stitch. 8cm wide.

Tape Laces

Lace constructed from pre-made tapes, without a net background, was made as early as the 1600s, but the heyday of tape laces was the second half of the nineteenth century when manufacturers produced an amazing variety of tapes. Two types of tape lace made commercially in the nineteenth century – Branscombe and Borris – have been described in Chapter 6, but many more tape laces were made by amateurs. Small thread buttons, rings and machine-embroidered medallions were often sold to be included in the lace. Every company seems to have had its own name for the patterns and the tapes it was selling, which makes things very confusing if you are relying on written sources. We have seen the names: Modern Lace; Venetian Point; Point Lace; Lacet work; Limoges Lace; Renaissance Lace; Bruges Lace; Honiton Lace;

English Lace; Russian Lace; Roman Lace, Battenberg and more. Sometimes these names seem to have been taken from the names of the braids they used, others because they had a vague look of handmade lace of the same name, but most names seem to have been plucked from the air. Faced with this level of confusion we are making no attempt to identify every variety and will concentrate on a few distinctive types.

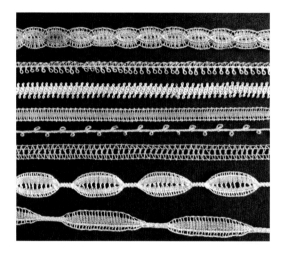

A small selection of machine-made tapes used for different tape laces. Tapes such as these were sold by the yard or made up into kits with threads and a pattern. Assistants in haberdashery departments were expected to work examples to display, and demonstrate techniques to potential customers.

Dickel lace is a tape lace that was first marketed in Germany early in the twentieth century. Patterns were produced for curtains, tablecloths and other furnishings assembled from simple tapes held together with buttonholed bars. These oddments were left over from a project bought from the Fenwick's department store in Newcastle upon Tyne (England) in the 1930s.

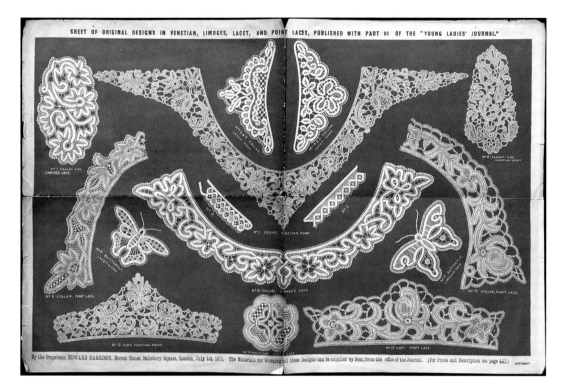

This large pattern sheet (77cm × 58cm) was a supplement in the July 1871 issue of *The Young Ladies' Journal*. All the patterns are for tape laces, which are given a variety of names. Examples with the same name do appear to have the same sort of tape and stitching. A sheet like this also provides useful information about styles of collars fashionable in the 1870s, and this can help with dating collars worked in other techniques.

Tape lace patterns were often printed on glazed cotton and sold with the necessary threads and tapes. This is the back panel (30cm × 40cm) of a large collar pattern, described as Honiton lace. It bears no relation to Honiton bobbin lace, but the main tape required is a string of leaf-shapes which was marketed as Honiton tape. A narrow unshaped tape was also needed. Tapes would be tacked to the pattern, then the connecting bars, with picots, worked. When complete the tacking threads were clipped to release the collar.

Some of the tape lace designs would have been relatively quick and satisfying to work, others, such as this example, would have been exceedingly tedious. This is one of the saddest pieces in our collections; it is the pattern for a tape-lace collar, composed mainly of small Honiton tape with a needle lace filling. The maker has tacked the tapes to one area, worked a small section of needle lace (about 9cm × 2.5cm) and then lost heart. Not surprising really as it must be one of the most boring patterns to work, and would probably not have been particularly attractive if it had ever been finished.

This is a tape collar that has been successfully completed. Two types of tapes have been used – one plain, the other scalloped – connected by two simple stitches: small woven spiders and Russian stitch.

Battenberg

This is one of the simpler of the tape laces. It was particularly popular with ladies in the USA at the beginning of the 1900s and the special tapes needed became available again towards the end of the twentieth century. Battenberg tapes are made in two styles and different widths; cords along the edges allow the tapes to be pulled up into smooth curves.

Battenberg tapes are widely used today in a variety of souvenir items such as fans and parasols. This one has a radius of just 20cm – it is too small to be useful, but looks good alongside a doll. Similar parasols in different sizes are now being marketed for weddings, sometimes dyed in bright colours and with matching fans. This parasol is well made, assembled from several lengths of plain Battenberg tape, using a combination of machine stitching to hold the embroidered panels in place, and simple needle lace stitches to link the braids. Courtesy Sheila Goldsworthy.

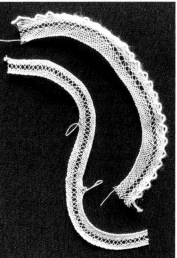

The handkerchief corner uses the two types of Battenberg tapes shown on the right, and also includes neatly worked needle lace fillings and a machine-embroidered panel recording it as a souvenir from Ostend.

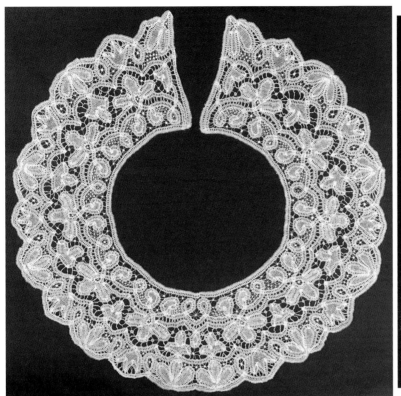

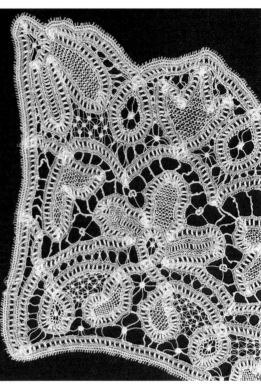

The tape used for this circular collar (detail on the right) is unusual, woven as it is like a long ladder. When the tape was sold it was possibly described as a Honiton Insertion. Another machine-made element is the picot edging. The collar was almost certainly made by an amateur who enjoyed experimenting with needle lace stitches to link the tapes and fill the spaces.

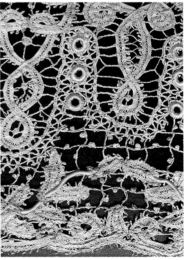

This triangle was presumably cut from a larger piece of fabric. It has been assembled from a variety of machine-made elements, including one tape that is used straight, a heavy cord, rings and the twisted threads with picots that form the background grid. The detail on the right shows three different tapes curling around to make the main features; one is very open, the other two are standard plain tapes of different weights – both of these have picots along one edge. A few small woven spiders and other simple stitching hold the lace together.

Tapes and Crochet

The tape laces described earlier in this chapter have all been assembled using a needle and thread, but there are a large number of laces that combine tapes with crochet.

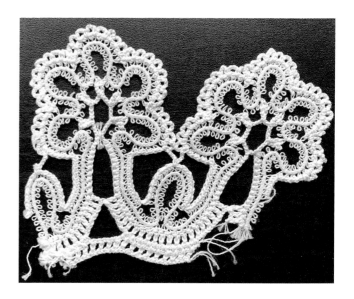

It is harder to see the tape in this pair of flowers: it is a cord with picots on each side. The rest of the lace is crochet. Height 7cm.

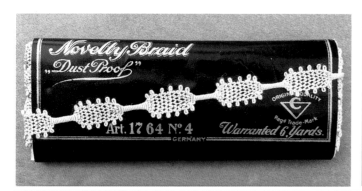

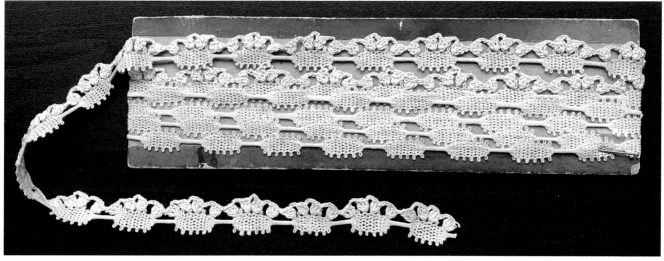

The 'novelty braid' in the packet (top left) was intended to be enhanced by crochet such as that shown on the right and below.

If you come across a lace that doesn't appear to fit into a regular category, look for a tape; it is surprising how often you will find one. This table mat appears to be all crochet and it is only when looking closely that it is possible to see that the 5.5cm diameter flower centres are made of a rickrack braid.

It is easier to see the rickrack braid in this enlarged image.

It is equally hard to spot the small rickrack braid in this tray-cloth border.

Portion of a crochet border combining two lengths of 'novelty braid' and a patterned tape with open-work edges.

Group of mid-twentieth-century booklets for craft laces, with some of the laces and their tools.

CHAPTER 8

CRAFT LACES

Craft laces are laces, or lace-like fabrics, that are made by hand using techniques that are neither bobbin nor needle lace. In the nineteenth and early twentieth centuries there were a number of small industries producing these laces for sale, but much more was made in the home for domestic or personal use. Most of the techniques that we might describe as craft laces can be found in Therese de Dillmont's *Encyclopedia of Needlework*, which was first published by DMC in 1886 – and is still in print. Most editions of the book are in a chunky format: 14cm × 10cm and 4.5cm deep. There are a few editions in a larger format, but these do not all contain the full range of techniques – which include bobbin and needle lace, lace knitting, crochet, macramé, netting, appliqué and darned net in addition to many other textile crafts.

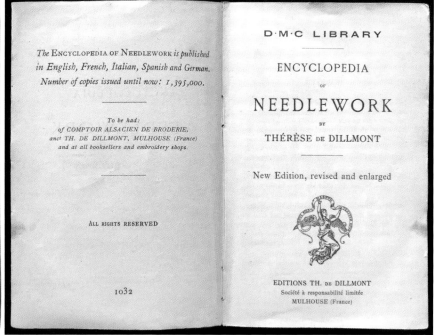

The front cover of a 1912 edition of the DMC *Encyclopedia of Needlework*, with the imprint of an embroidery shop in Glasgow on the left and the title pages of a 1932 edition on the right. We can work out the date of publication by the number at the bottom of the left hand page: this is 1032, which indicates it was published in the tenth month of 1932. The number in the earlier book is 412, which shows that it was published in the fourth month of 1912. Many DMC publications can be dated in this way.

A twentieth-century Shetland shawl, worked in 1-ply Shetland wool. This 120cm square shawl was started with the long outside border – a total of 480cm – which was joined by grafting start to finish at one corner.

Knitting

Knitted lace is a looped fabric constructed from a single continuous thread. For hand knitting, the tools are a pair (or more) of pointed needles, while machine knitting involves a frame and one or more rows of small latchet hooks. Knitting has a long history, but knitted lace did not appear until the end of the eighteenth century when it was worked in silk for stockings. Throughout the Victorian period, and well into the twentieth century, lace was knitted in linen then cotton for clothing and household items such as tablecloths, doilies and towel edgings.

Lace knitting using fine wool from the native sheep began

in Shetland in the 1830s and soon become fashionable in London, with the trade continuing for more than eighty years. Shawls were the main product, together with a range of baby and children's clothing and underwear – helped by the idea that knitted garments were good for health. 'Gossamer Shawls' from Orenburg in Russia, knitted with yarn spun from the undercoat of native goats, have a similar history.

The finest of Shetland shawls can be pulled through a wedding ring and were so delicate that the knitters needed to avoid any work that might roughen their hands. These shawls are rarely made today, as there are few people who can spin the very fine wool required. We might expect Shetland shawls to be white or cream, but many were made in strong colours – typically black, red or purple. Traditionally the stitch patterns – which often had local names, such as fern, faggot border, print o' the wave – were passed down the generations and there were no printed patterns. With clever planning and use of a grafting technique the construction of a shawl can be accomplished with very little in the way of casting on and off, which minimizes the number of hard lines.

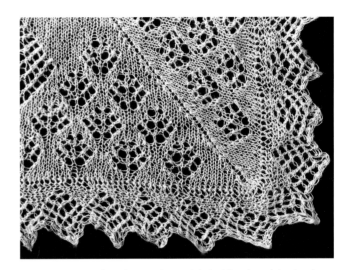

The hundreds of stitches on the straight inside edge of the border were picked up on a long circular needle. Knitting was then worked from the outside in, reducing the number of stitches on either side of each corner. Stitches were transferred to four or five needles when there were too few stitches to work on a circular needle.

From the 1940s to the 1970s, patterns designed by Marianne Kinzel – a refugee from Czechoslovakia – were widely available, first under the name 'Viennese Lace', then 'Modern Lace Knitting'. Most of her patterns are for household items. This mat is the plate-size doily (12cm across) from the Azalea luncheon set in Kinzel's *First Book of Modern Lace Knitting*. Note the doily has been knitted in the round, starting in the middle with a few stitches and adding stitches as the rounds get longer. Like most mats of this type, the outer edge has been finished with a crochet chain.

In the Azores doilies are knitted from pita thread, a fibre extracted from the agave plant. This example was produced in the twentieth century for the tourist market. (17cm diameter) Courtesy Lilian McCormick.

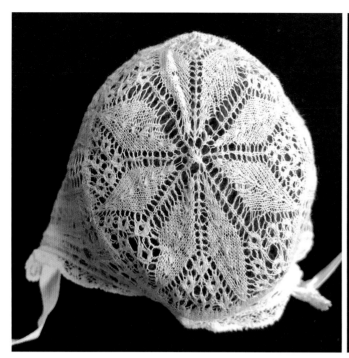

This baby's bonnet is tiny: the back is just 8cm across, knitted from the centre like a doily. On the right the knitted panel that goes around the head is 9cm wide. Both sections show a variety of open stitches, and the whole is trimmed by a machine-made Valenciennes edging.

There is a little knitted jacket that goes with the bonnet. It is a slightly odd shape (total width 44cm, depth 15cm, 22cm sleeve) but very stretchy so would probably fit well on a wriggly baby. (A similar set of knitted jacket and bonnet with machine-lace trim is in the Museum of Applied Arts in Budapest, dated 1898.)

Crochet

Crochet is constructed from a single continuous thread using a hook to work interconnected loop stitches. The craft evolved in the nineteenth century from tambour work where a hook is used to work chain stitch on stretched fabric. From the start, crochet has been used to produce lacy fabrics. The heyday was the Victorian period across all levels of society. Crochet is easy to transport, to pick up and put down. It is also robust and washes well, which made it particularly popular with Travellers for curtains and domestic linens in their narrow boats and caravans. Crochet on table linen was one of very few laces that would have come to little harm when subjected to the drastic washing methods – such as simmering for several hours in a solution of borax and soap – that were still advocated at the beginning of the twentieth century.

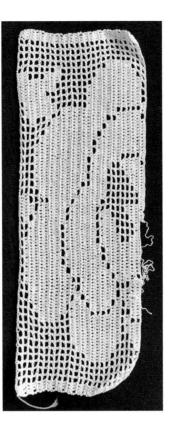

A distinct style of crochet is filet crochet, mentioned in Chapter 2 as one of laces you are likely to find on household and church linens. Filet crochet designs are based on small squares that can be either filled or open. The lace is worked in rows from edge to edge and can be easily drafted on squared paper or by adapting a cross-stitch pattern. This short sample shows the first few rows of a wide border for an altar cloth – the rose design is beginning to appear. 23cm wide.

Irish crochet

The making of crochet was one of the industries established in Ireland during the potato blight in the 1840s. The crochet style adopted was one that attempted to mimic seventeenth-century needle lace. The lace was made as separate motifs – mainly flowers, often with raised petals, and leaves of various shapes including shamrocks. The motifs were then usually linked by crochet bars with picots (known as clones knots). Collars, cuffs and even complete jackets and dresses were made, unfortunately good design was often lacking and many pieces appear to have been assembled from a random collection of motifs.

Many crochet items are assembled from motifs, with the pineapple motif being very popular. The pattern for this doily can be found in a Coats booklet published in the 1960s, which also has patterns for pineapple tablecloths and a bedspread – the latter composed of dozens of pineapples, requiring 146 balls of no.20 crochet cotton.

This is a densely worked Irish crochet collar composed of numerous square units, each centred on a small flower or leaf, surrounded by clones knots (chains with picots). The squares can just be distinguished in the image of the central area of the collar on the nest page. Most of the flowers have raised petals and the whole collar is finished with an edging of small scallops.

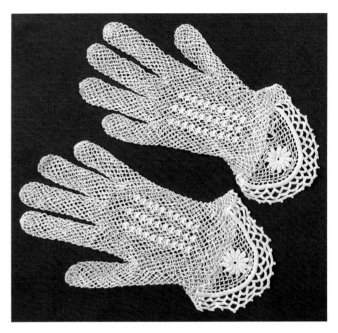

This collar might have been made by one person, but it is more likely that several workers were involved. For example with one person making the large flowers while others made the square units, other workers would then connect the units and work the scalloped edging. In this way a large item could be completed at speed, often with most of the work carried out in the workers' homes.

Crochet gloves from Brittany – the edging and daisy (*paquerette*) motif are typical of Picot Bigouden.

The overall design of this collar is well balanced with leaf and flower motifs on either side of the central web. The delicate flower motifs that surround the web are carefully worked, as is the scalloped edge – the same edging as the long collar – and there are small areas of clones knots. However the flowers and leaves that form the main elements are clumsy in their design and execution and do little to add to the look of the whole piece.

Irish crochet elsewhere

At the beginning of the twentieth century, Irish crochet was also introduced to other parts of Europe with the aim of providing employment. In Brittany where the lace became known as Picot Bigouden, the lace industry was started in 1903 to provide relief during a crisis in the Breton sardine fishing industry. Similar lace industries to support working-class women were set up, often by wealthy patrons, in other areas including Orvieto in central Italy and Csetnek in Hungary. The lace made in all these places used Irish crochet techniques but the introduction of local designs and motifs meant that each lace developed its own individual style, with its own name (for example Merletto di Orvieto and Cestnek Csipke).

Romanian Point

Also known as Hungarian Point, this is worked in the same way as a tape lace, with crochet tapes (braids) and needle lace fillings. The technique dates from early in the twentieth century, probably originating in France, then spreading to many parts of Europe, Egypt and America. It is still made for sale in Romania.

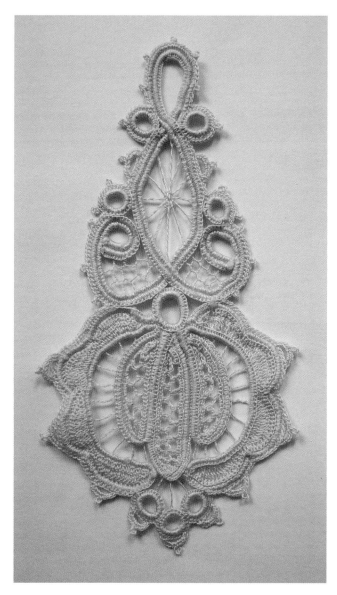

Reproduction of a Csetnek lace motif, based on an old pattern. The spider filling in the oval and the stitches in the two spaces at either side of it are needle lace, worked after the crochet is finished. The addition of needle lace fillings is a feature of Csetnek crochet. (10.5 × 5.5cm) Courtesy Laura Czegledi.

The basic Romanian braid provides the crochet outlines in this small mat, designed and worked by Pat Brunsden. Needle-weaving is used to make the inner motifs – known as wheat-ears – and the other filling and connecting stitches are needle lace.

Hairpin Crochet

This method of crochet starts with a braid worked over the prongs of a U-shaped former. If working with fine thread this can be an actual hairpin; a larger former is needed for thicker thread. The braid has a solid centre and loops on each side. Standard crochet techniques are used to connect the braids, picking up groups of loops to create mats, shawls and other items. This style of crochet was popular in the 1960s and 70s.

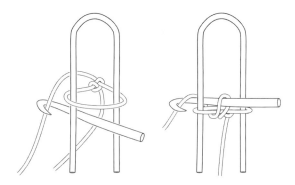

Starting a braid with loops around the prongs of a hairpin. (The braid can also be worked with the hairpin the other way up.)

Three lengths of hairpin braid make up this small mat. One gives the inner ring, with the loops on one side pulled together to form the centre, the loops on the other side of the braid are linked with a crochet chain to the loops of a second braid. The outer braid is gathered into shallow scallops as it is linked with chains to the middle braid.

Tatting

The origin of tatting is knotting with a shuttle, a craft that was popular in the eighteenth century, when ladies used the movements of the shuttle to show off their hands at social occasions. (The resulting strings of knots were used for fringes, tassels or couched embroideries.)

Tatting evolved in the first half of the nineteenth century when rings composed of lark's head knots decorated with picots first appeared. These were used as edgings or stitched, or tied together to form larger items. Mlle Riego de la Branchardiere is credited with developing the craft further, introducing a knotted arc, known as a chain, instead of just a thread between rings, (see pink chains with picots in the tatted motif in Chapter 1), and using picots to link rings and chains as the tatting was worked. She won prizes at the 1851 Great Exhibition and published eleven books between 1850 and 1868 that show gradual changes in the craft. Like many craft laces, tatting suffered a decline in the first half of the twentieth century, with a brief revival in the 1950s. Twenty-first century tatters are now experimenting with a wide variety of new techniques including split-rings, complex bars, use of beads and tatting with a needle.

The tatting shuttle is being used to work a row of small rings linked with picots. The little 'flowers' on the left are made by working very long picots between the stitches of the ring.

A twentieth-century tatted mat worked in crochet cotton. The basic stitch is a larks-head knot and the main design features are rings and curved bars (known as chains) decorated with small picots. Picots are both decorative and functional as they serve to link different elements.

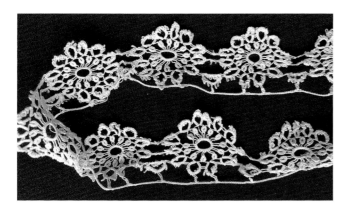

This early example of tatting consists of ten rosettes composed of rings with picots – there are no chains, instead a single thread goes from one ring to the next. The rosettes have been tied together through adjacent picots to form a small cuff. Each rosette is 2cm across.

Netting and Knotting

Filet

The knotting of nets for fishing and trapping is one of the oldest textile crafts. In the sixteenth century the craft was miniaturized with square-mesh nets becoming the base of a decorative fabric that is now known as filet or lacis. Squares of knotted mesh worked in linen thread were decorated with running stitch to create simple motifs or complex pictures. Large hangings and covers have survived where squares of filet are set between linen panels.

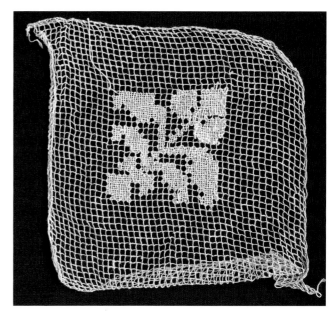

A square of hand-knotted net, darned with a simple motif – the darning goes four times across each mesh (up, down, left to right and right to left). The square has relaxed towards a diamond shape due to its construction method: starting at a corner with a single mesh, adding one mesh per row to the required width then reducing again to a point. The net is usually stretched in a rigid frame for darning. Sides are 13cm.

An elaborate design, probably worked in the nineteenth century in imitation of the sixteenth-century panels that were often complex illustrations of biblical or classical stories. 18cm square.

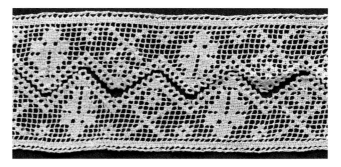

This nineteenth-century edging has been planned to allow two lengths of filet to be worked on one length of knotted net. Each piece is 3cm wide; the mesh is just 2mm square.

Guipure d'Art

Filet went out of favour in the 1700s when bobbin and needle lace had reached a high level of development, but there was a revival of interest towards the end of the nineteenth century. At that time more varied embroidery stitches were introduced on a relatively large square mesh. This type of work gained the name of Guipure d'Art, and was used mainly for furnishings.

A net with a 5mm square mesh is used for the background of this Guipure d'Art mat. Most of the pattern is simple darning with extra decoration created by taking threads across the surface. 43cm × 30cm.

Netting with varied mesh

The size of the mesh in a piece of netting is determined by the size of the mesh stick used. By using different sizes of mesh it is possible to produce a decorative net that needs no additional embroidery. A variety of items can be found that have been made in this way.

Macramé

Macramé is the name given to a technique of knotting multiple threads to produce an openwork fabric. Although usually made with cords that can be easily manipulated with the fingers, macramé can also be worked with finer threads, such as the warp threads from a piece of weaving, to produce an open fabric. This is a technique widely used in Crete to finish the ends of their ceremonial towels.

A version of macramé known as Margaretenspitze, which includes three-dimensional items, was developed in Germany during the first quarter of the twentieth century.

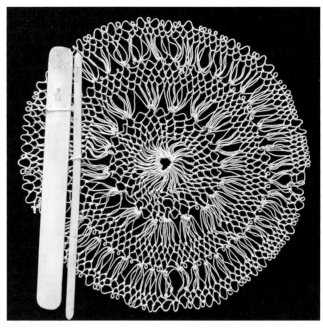

The doily shown was worked using two sizes of mesh stick, in this case 9/16 of an inch and 3/16. Any smooth stick can be used as a mesh stick but the serious netter often had a set of different sizes. These ones are bone.

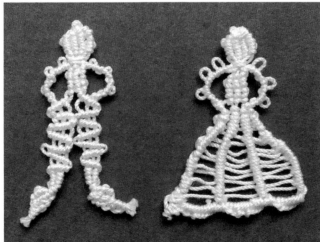

The single figure (7cm high) on the left was worked using standard macramé techniques. The pair of figures (4cm high) on the right are *Margaretenspitze*.

Tenerife and Ñandutí

Tenerife is an embroidered lace composed almost entirely of circular medallions worked with a variety of stitches over a radial web. The lace has its origins as a way of filling the corner space where both warp and weft threads have been removed from fabric in a piece of cutwork, or drawn-work embroidery. Tenerife, also known as Sol Lace, has been widely made in Spain and in South America where a particularly delicate version of the lace, known as Ñandutí, is still made in Paraguay and often worked in coloured threads today.

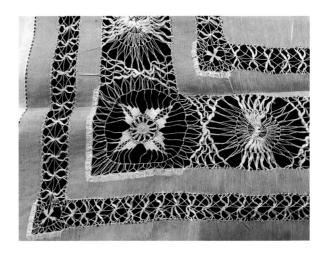

The drawn-thread embroidery on this silk cloth shows clearly the origin of Tenerife lace. Multiple threads have been drawn out of three concentric squares leaving empty spaces in the corners and vertical threads along the sides. In the narrow bands these threads have been pulled into groups. The detail of a corner shows where additional threads have been laid and rosettes of needle-weaving worked. Courtesy Vivien Boulton.

Ñandutí is usually worked with silk or fine cotton and in contrast to Tenerife, the whole design is marked out on a fabric pattern with small tacking stitches to support the initial web of spokes. This allows the easy working of more varied shapes, for example the large wheels that make up the main part of this collar are not all circular – their shape has been adjusted to fit the space available. Between the wheels are smaller shapes, with small scallops all round the outer edges. In this piece no attempt has been made at exact symmetry in the working of the wheels or filler shapes. Back panel is 12cm × 18cm, overall length 51cm.

It is always helpful when a piece of lace comes with its original label. This one has in tiny writing the word Tenerife – the country where it was made – and it is the type of work known as Tenerife. In this case the lace has a central needle-woven star surrounded by eight needle-woven flowers, each worked over a radial web of threads.

Some of the stages in working Ruskin lace on even-weave linen can be seen in this part-worked needle case. The process starts with the withdrawing of horizontal threads to form the borders, then vertical threads are pulled together by hem-stitching. Threads are completely cut out from a central square which is oversewn around the edge and the centre filled with needle lace, including buttonholed arcs and circles with picots, triangles of closely worked buttonhole stitches and an eight-point star of twisted threads. 39cm × 18.5cm.

Embroidered Lace

Ruskin lace is a form of cutwork embroidery. In 1833 John Ruskin with support from the Guild of St George set up an industry in Cumbria for women to spin then weave locally grown flax. As the quality of the linen improved, the industry expanded to include made-up and embroidered items. By the end of the nineteenth century most of the embroidery was a simplified version of the sixteenth century cutwork where areas of the fabric are cut away and filled with embroidery stitches. This work was at that time called 'Greek lace', but has since become known as Ruskin lace and has continued as a leisure activity after the demise of hand-woven linen. Related openwork embroideries include Lefkara, Hardanger and Hedebo.

Closely related to Ruskin lace is this Lefkara lace mat made in Cyprus in the 1990s. Corners are 5cm squares of reticella needle lace worked with a heavy thread, which is also used for the drawn thread work across the mat and the needle lace edging. (28cm × 39cm) Courtesy Diane Cooper.

Broderie Anglaise

This is a whitework embroidery, not really a lace but often used where lace might otherwise be found – mainly children's clothes, underwear and household linens. The method of working can be seen in the unfinished length. The initial patterning is usually done with an embroidery machine with additional embroidery worked by hand. Metal stamps may be used to mark the stitching lines for scallops and other features.

The little disc of Ayrshire whitework (6.5cm diameter), intended for the back of a baby's bonnet, contains small circles of twisted buttonhole stitch.

In this piece of Broderie Anglaise the holes, outline stitches and the grid in the larger spaces have been worked with an embroidery machine. The irregularities indicate that the rest of the embroidery, including the buttonholed scallops, was worked by hand. This piece still needs to be finished by trimming around the scallops. Scallops are 3cm across.

Ayrshire whitework

This is also usually classed as embroidery, but the best Ayrshire work includes areas of needle lace, while the delicacy of the fine cotton lawn used, together with the extensive pierced work in the designs, gives the whole a lace-like look. Ayrshire, where most of the embroidery was done, is a county just south of Glasgow. When the craft was at its height between 1820 and 1860 this area was a centre for the manufacture of very fine cotton fabric. Ayrshire work is too delicate for household linens; it has been used for items such as handkerchiefs and collars, but most of the production was baby clothing with the long dresses known as robes being a speciality.

The fragment of whitework, possibly part of a tippet or other shoulder covering, has a greater variety of embroidery in the design, including many tiny flowers with open centres and two larger flowers with oval spaces filled with simple needle lace. Larger areas with more varied needle lace stitches can be found in robes, collars and decorative panels.

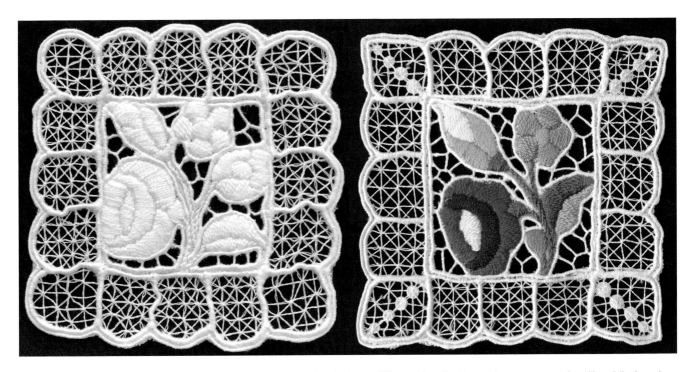

The two 10cm coasters of Kalosca lace are very similar in structure, but look very different. The all-white version appears very lace-like while the colour in the second one emphasizes the embroidery. Courtesy Elaine Williams.

Kalosca Lace

This embroidered lace has been made in the Hungarian district of Kalosca since the early 1900s, initially for the colourful local costume, but now also for the tourist market. The initial stage is to work the padded satin-stitch embroidery on white cotton, before using a domestic sewing machine to outline the rest of the design. Fabric is then cut away from inside the outlines and the sewing machine used again to work the criss-cross grids within the spaces. The final stage is to work close zigzag stitching to strengthen all the outlines.

Long, black machine-lace stole, mid-nineteenth century.

CHAPTER 9

MACHINE LACE

Is it machine made?

From its start the aim of the machine lace industry was to copy handmade lace, particularly bobbin lace. In this it has been extremely successful and as a result it is often difficult to separate hand from machine. The following pointers would indicate that a lace is machine made.

1. All-over woven look.
2. Extreme regularity of appearance.
3. No errors or the same error on every repeat.
4. A fuzzy appearance, difficulty in following the course of threads.
5. A ribbed effect.
6. Very wide piece with no sign of a join.
7. A separate strip of picots stitched to the edge.

A Brief History of Machine Lace

Nets

As early as 1589 a Nottinghamshire clergyman (William Lee) invented a knitting frame (also called a stocking frame) that was used for the next 200 years for knitting items such as caps and stockings. Initially only coarse wool could be used, but refinements allowed work with finer yarns such as silk. Later, small areas of open stitches could be incorporated and in 1786 a six-sided mesh, known as point-net, was achieved. The early knitted nets had two major disadvantages: as with any knitted fabric they were a) stretchy, and b) inclined to

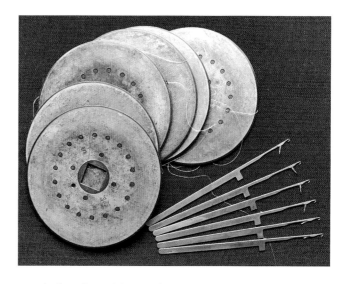

Hooked needles with latchets from a knitting machine and some of the very slim thread holders from the carriages of a bobbinet machine. These discs are 6cm in diameter and 1mm thick, each composed of two thinner disks with a gap between, where a fine thread is wound.

run into holes if a thread was snagged. Heavy dressing was needed to counteract those problems. Very little early knitted net has survived and it is highly unlikely that you will find any outside a specialist museum.

The real breakthrough in net came in 1808 when John Heathcoat invented a machine that could replicate the hexagonal mesh made by bobbin lacemakers (point ground – see Chapter 3). The first net was very narrow, but a year later Heathcoat had a machine that could make cotton net, known as bobbinet, up to thirty inches wide (90cm). Bobbinet keeps its shape and does not run, and is the background for most of the net-based laces described in Chapter 7.

Heathcoat's patent expired in 1821 and the industry

exploded with numerous innovations and hundreds of home-workers producing 'brown net', which was passed to the lace manufacturers for finishing and embroidery. In England Nottingham became an increasingly important centre with production and distribution activities gathered into large premises. Designers were added to the teams as lace became more complicated and needed to respond rapidly to the demands of ever changing fashion. There were similar industries in France, Switzerland and Austria. The development of machines that could make delicate lace was matched by rapidly developing skills among the engineers and inventors who had the imagination and technical expertise to make the parts and put the machines together.

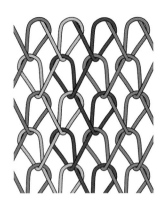

Structure of basic warp knitting; each of the coloured lines represents one thread, which is linked to adjacent threads as the lace is worked upwards.

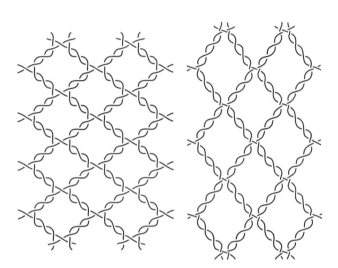

The diagram on the left is bobbinet with the hexagonal mesh replicating point ground in bobbin lace: two threads cross at top and bottom of each mesh and there are two threads twisted three times on each of the other four sides. Confusingly this is described in the industry as a 2-twist net while the diamond-shaped mesh on the right is described as a 3-twist net – these descriptions refer to the number of movements made by a machine as it makes one mesh.

Warp frame knitting – Raschel machine

The structure of the fabric produced on a stocking frame is similar to that produced by hand knitting; horizontal rows of loops constructed from a single thread. Warp knitting is more like crochet with vertical lines of loops each worked with a separate thread and the fabric created by exchanging loops between the vertical lines. Large quantities of patterned nets were made on warp knitting machines in the period 1800 to

1840 and the manufacturers were among the first to adopt jacquard cards to control the pattern.

The Raschel machine is a modification of the warp frame that allows the addition of extra threads to be woven – not knitted – into the fabric to form a wide variety of patterned laces. Raschel machines came into use in the 1850s, fell out of favour around the turn of the century, and came back with modifications in the 1950s often using the new nylon and polyester threads. Under magnification the looped structure of a knitted fabric can be seen in all Raschel laces. Machine-

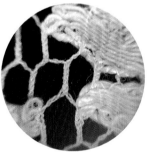

A 6cm-wide border made on a Raschel machine. The threads filling the motifs are woven in at the same time as the mesh is formed. The basic looped structure, visible in the enlarged image, is warp knitting – looped stitches which provide the background mesh.

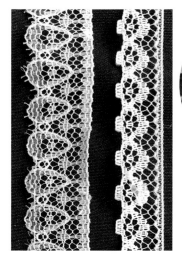

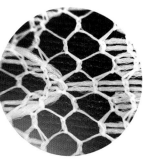

Two narrow edgings (1.1cm and 1.8cm wide) made with synthetic yarn on a Raschel machine. The chain stitch structure that holds the woven threads in place can be seen in the enlarged detail.

knitted scarves and shawls are likely to have been produced on a Raschel machine, as are many of the lace trimmings marketed today.

Pusher machine

The Pusher machine, patented in 1825, is a modified form of the bobbinet machine with a mechanism that pushes thread carriages into different positions to work patterned areas. Until jacquard cards were introduced in 1834 it was a relatively slow machine and the lace required considerable hand finishing, which made the lace expensive. Pusher machines were the first to copy half stitch and they became known for their imitation Chantilly, particularly the large shawls which were worked in silk, mohair or fine wool. These were fashionable between 1850 and 1870. In 1875 the machines were adapted to produce Spanish Blondes in cream, black and white. Lyons was the main centre for this. The black lace stole illustrated at the start of this chapter was made on a Pusher machine, which produced both the mesh background and the denser areas. The thicker outlines were then run in by hand with a needle and thread.

JACQUARD CARDS

In 1804 Joseph Jacquard invented a system of punched cards to control the lifting of warp threads when weaving complex patterns. The system requires a continuous band of cards which moves round as the weaving progresses. Each set of holes controls one part of a pattern repeat. When a punched hole passes a specific part of the mechanism it triggers the lifting of a thread; if there is no hole at that position the thread is not lifted. Lace machines are usually more complex than looms so it was thirty years before jacquard cards could control lace machines. On a

Pusher machine as many as 5,000 jacquard cards might be needed to produce a large shawl with a complex pattern. As with weaving, the introduction of jacquard cards considerably reduced the amount of labour required and therefore the price of the finished item. Computers are gradually replacing jacquard cards for controlling lace machines, which is a neat circle of innovation since Charles Babbage, recognized as the father of computing, used jacquard cards as his inspiration for the punch cards of his first computers.

This 67cm long jacquard card is from the MYB Textiles factory in Ayrshire. There is an arrangement of small holes that is repeated three times across the card, which indicates that when the card is in use it would be controlling one small part of three identical lengths of loom lace. Note there is a number towards the left of the card which indicates the position the card would be on the continuous band that controlled the machine; the band is made by threading cords through the rows of four holes across the card. The largest holes control the position of the card as it passes through the machine.

The nearly square mesh, ribbed effect in the clothwork and small areas of decorative fillings visible in this image are all typical of Pusher lace. The end of the stole also shows the machine-made picot strip on the edge (detached in places). One of the motifs in the detail on the right is missing the outline thread. This is a strong indication that the stole was made between 1830, when the patterning was possible, but outlines needed to be put in by hand, and the 1840s, when machines could also put in the outline threads. Width is 50cm, total length 250cm.

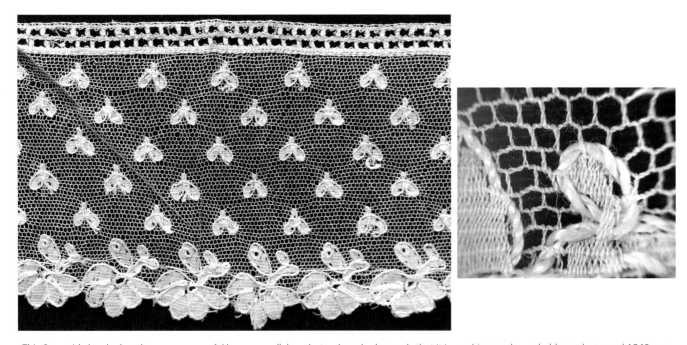

This 6cm-wide border has the appearance of Alençon needlelace, but a closer look reveals that it is machine made, probably made around 1840 on a Pusher machine. The initial clues are the closely packed threads in the clothwork areas visible with the naked eye. In the magnified detail on the right the twisted threads of the square mesh are visible and it is clear that the outline threads have been needle-run in and out of the lace. (The horizontal thread towards the headside is not part of the lace and it is unclear why it is there.)

OUTLINE THREADS

Many types of lace include a thicker outlining thread. In bobbin lace this is known as a gimp and is usually added as a pair, giving a neat start to a feature. At the finish the gimp threads are crossed over and cut off, leaving two little ends. These can be seen in the Chantilly veil shown in Chapter 3, where the outline gimp has been cut off after every spot. Early lace machines could work patterned net, but could not include the outline threads, which had to be added by hand. Workers known as 'lace runners' used a needle and long lengths of thread to put in the outlines by hand, stitching in and out of the mesh, working round features in directions that would be impossible in bobbin lace. After 1841, machines could put in the outline as the lace was worked. The thicker threads, known as liners, were carried loosely from one motif to the next and clipped when the lace came off the machine. This process leaves short ends at the start as well as finish of each feature.

(Another form of outline thread is attached by a sewing machine that couches the thread to one surface of the lace. This is very obvious when it is possible to view the lace from both sides.)

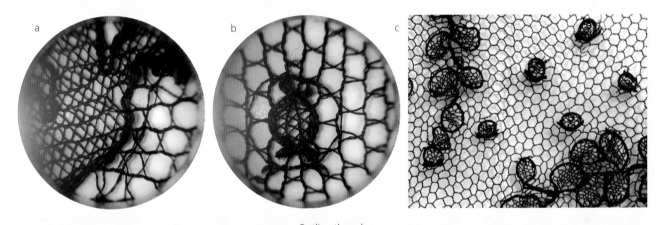

Outline threads:
a. threads are needle-run by hand after lace comes off the machine
b. threads inserted as the machine lace is made
c. gimps around the spots in handmade Chantilly lace

Cornely machine

A form of embroidery machine known as the Cornely or Bonnaz was introduced in 1865. This is a small machine that can be used in the home or small workshop to stitch an outline or complete design by chain stitching a fine cord on the surface of plain or patterned net.

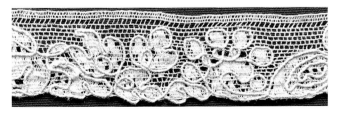

Raised outlines applied by a Cornely machine on a length of Pusher lace.

A small section of an all-over lace fabric patterned entirely by simple motifs, composed of a continuous thread couched to one surface by a Cornely machine, which puts a barely visible chain stitch at the back of the net.

Leavers machine

First patented in 1828 the Leavers machine is a modification of Heathcoat's bobbinet machine. Over the next hundred years many different mesh structures were developed (and used extensively for fancy hat veils) alongside imitations of virtually every variety of bobbin lace. Leavers machines are large and can produce all-over patterns, either to be used as lace fabric or separated into individual motifs or lengths. Multiple copies of insertions and edgings are worked back-to-back, linked by easily removed lacer threads. Lacer threads may also be used to support picots along the edges. For economy, scallops are usually designed to fit neatly in the spaces between the scallops of an adjacent lace.

Diagram showing arrangement of four edgings linked with lacer threads.

The ridged effect of the clothwork and the rather messy bars in this bookmark are typical of one style of lace made on a Leavers machine. The cut ends suggest that the three squares were cut from strips of a wide piece of fabric and no lacer threads were involved. (It is fairly safe to assume that a label of this type is correct.)

This doily made on a Levers machine has the same ridged effect and irregular bars as the bookmark. It would have been cut from a wide piece of fabric before adding the edging of crochet chains.

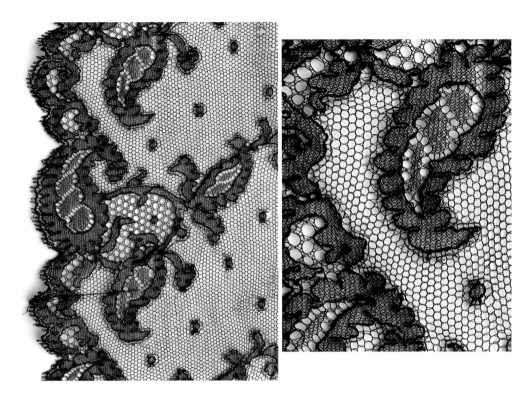

It is not always easy to see the detail of black lace and this 13cm wide border could easily be thought of as bobbin lace. However there are several factors visible with the naked eye that indicate it is machine made: the clothwork has a distinctly ribbed effect, the picots are rather long and the outline threads around the dots have cut ends at top and bottom. The background mesh is hexagonal like that of bobbinet. Without magnification the filling stitch looks like honeycomb, but in the magnified image on the right the arrangement of threads can be seen to be completely different. The imitation half stitch has diagonal lines, but instead of the horizontal threads that would be found in bobbin-made half stitch, the dominant threads run lengthwise along the lace.

The rather wispy look along the headside means that it is relatively easy to recognize this border as machine made. Stitch structure is similar to the previous example, but the threads used for the clothwork are softer and the headside is quite weak, with the cut edge of the scallops very noticeable below the stitched-on picot strip. 14cm wide.

It is likely that this large centrepiece (38cm diameter) was made to mark the coronation of Queen Elizabeth II in 1953. The lace has the fine square mesh typical of that made on a curtain net machine with the pattern entirely compsed of squares that are either open or filled by close weaving.

This doily (26cm diameter) is an example of machine-woven Madras lace. The detail shows where the soft filler threads have been cut after being carried during the weaving process as floaters from one part of the design to the next.

Curtain machine

Lace made on the curtain machine can be recognized by the square mesh. Lace curtains were a novelty in the 1840s when the curtain machine was first developed in Nottingham (quickly spreading to France, Poland, Russia and America). The Nottingham curtain industry remained profitable until early in the twentieth century, when houses were being built with smaller windows and there was increasing competition from America. However, the machines could also make table cloths, bedspreads and fashion items such as collars and even complete dresses. In 1939 most of the production was diverted to the war effort producing vast quantities of camouflage, sand-fly and mosquito netting (coloured to suit the environment where it would be used). The machines can cope equally well with natural and synthetic fibres.

Loom lace

It is possible to produce a lace-like effect by manipulating the warp and/or weft threads on a hand loom, but this is more difficult on a mechanized one. However, there is one firm – Morton, Young and Borland, now known as MYB Textiles – which is based in Ayrshire, Scotland that specializes in creating a light, filmy fabric with the design formed from a soft cotton thread. The fabric is known as Madras lace and is marketed all over the world.

Barmen machine

Machines now known as Barmen machines were patented in the 1890s. These had evolved from braiding machines making braids for surface decoration, and then the numerous varieties of tape used for the tape laces described in Chapter 7. They have a natural diagonal weave that is easily adapted to copying Torchon and other geometric bobbin laces, with additional mechanisms needed for imitating other laces. The standard Barmen machine produces a maximum lace width of 8in (20cms) that is often made up of two or more narrow laces linked by nylon lacer threads. The machine works in a circular motion producing the lace as a tube, with the lacer threads withdrawn as the lace comes off the machine to separate it into flat lengths.

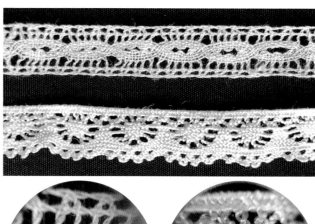

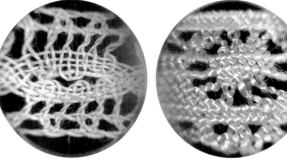

The heavier lace (4.5cm wide) in this illustration was bought in the 1970s from a Traveller who was in Newcastle for the annual Hoppings funfair; it was sold as handmade lace but was almost certainly made on a Barmen machine. The smaller sample is bobbin lace of a similar structure.

An insertion and narrow edging, each approximately 1cm wide, both made on Barmen machines. The insertion could easily be worked with bobbins, but it is much more likely to have been machine made for use in tape lace or as an engrelure. The edging with its shiny thread has much more of a 'machine-look'. Details of the insertion and the edging can be seen in the Phonescope images.

The square mesh ground in this piece makes it appear to be lace made on a curtain machine, but a close look shows that the ground is composed of twisted pairs and plaits – a mesh that can be produced by a Barmen machine – the tightly woven blocks are also common in Barmen lace. Width 8cm.

Embroidery Machines

The machines described in the first part of this chapter are good at copying bobbin laces, but not so good when it comes to imitating needle lace or craft laces such as crochet and tatting. For these an embroidery machine is required. The first of these machines came into use in 1829, and was the Handmachine, controlled by an operative with a pantograph. This could replicate numerous copies at a time of hand-embroidered motifs, using multiple needles each with an eye in the middle and a point at each end. It was entirely hand and foot controlled, and was a relatively expensive process with many designs requiring considerable hand finishing. Sixteen thousand of these machines were recorded in St Gallen, Switzerland in 1908, which explains the alternative name of Swiss machine. The machines were also in use in the USA, Germany and Poland.

During the 1880s a new type of embroidery machine – the Schiffli – began to replace the Handmachine; it was faster, more versatile and required less human input than the earlier machines. The embroidery is worked with two threads, one in a needle above the fabric and one in a shuttle below. The basic stitch is a lock stitch (the same stitch that is made by a standard home sewing machine today), which can be varied to create a variety of effects. Initially the Schiffli was used on net, producing imitations of needle and bobbin laces with net grounds, and on fine fabric where borers, incorporated

in the machines, could make holes allowing the imitation of handmade open-work such as Broderie Anglaise. For small holes the borer pushes through the fabric then the resulting hole is tightly oversewn; for larger holes the outline is stitched first, then a large borer is used, which snaps the threads of the fabric before the circle is oversewn.

Very good imitations of Broderie Anglaise can be made by a Schiffli machine. An example is this 3.5cm wide insertion photographed from the back to show where threads go from one part of the work to another. These threads are in identical positions on each repeat, which confirms that this is machine made.

Schiffli embroidery on net: this example has been worked on a curve so was possibly intended as the front edge of an open gown. The net has been cut away along a continuous line of stitching. Repeats are approx. 4cm.

Schiffli embroidery can capture the essence of a variety of bobbin and needle laces. This delicate doily (23cm across) could easily be mis-identified as a pieced bobbin lace such as Duchesse or Honiton applied to net.

Guipure laces had been difficult to copy until the development of chemical lace. The technique for this is to embroider the design on a disposable fabric, ensuring that all parts of the design are connected by stitching. A chemical that will dissolve the background fabric, but have no effect on the stitching thread, is then applied and the background dissolved away. (Embroiderers today use the same process with water-soluble fabric.)

Schiffli embroidery may be very delicate or be built up in multiple layers to create guipure fabrics, some in imitation of needle laces such as Gros Point and Point de Gaze, others in a form that is recognizable as lace, but bears little relationship to any named variety of handmade lace. The lace may be used as a whole fabric, or cut into individual motifs or groups of motifs for use as insertions or surface decoration.

 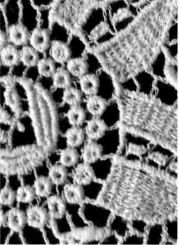

Most chemical lace has been embroidered with a Schiffli machine, and the lace can usually be recognized by the slightly fuzzy appearance produced by stitching over the top of stitching. 8.5cm wide. On the right a close-up of the embroidery shows there are layers of stitches.

A motif like this – probably intended as decoration for a lapel or similar – would have started life as one of hundreds of embroidered motifs on a wide length of disposable fabric. This piece (approximately 12cm × 9cm) is composed of flowers, leaves and bars with picots; it could be separated further into two flowers and two separate leaves, or a leaf with two flowers plus a separate leaf, or two leaves and a flower plus a separate flower. Cutting today might be by laser but it was originally done by hand and there are ledgers in the Nottingham lace archives that list the payment (per dozen or hundred) for each shape cut.

For a collar such as this, the Schiffli employs a variety of stitches giving different textures and using satin stitch to give maximum shine.

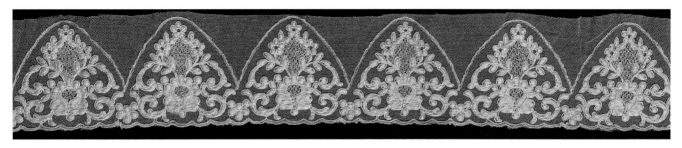

Similar stitches have been used in this coffee-coloured border, which shows the absolute regularity possible with a Schiffli machine. The lace has been trimmed close to the gently scalloped edge; the stitching on the other edge is more uneven and suggests this is a marker line to indicate where the border would be stitched to a wider piece of net or other fabric.

This is the rather sad remnant of a chemisette (see Chapter 11). Much of the fine fabric has torn away, while the Schiffli embroidery has survived. Most of the stitching is surface embroidery, but the area just below the neck has heavily stitched outlines with the spaces between cut away by hand. Short lengths of a machine-made Valenciennes have been stitched across the back of the two large spaces. (There is also a machine-made Valenciennes edging gathered slightly and hand stitched to the inside of the neckline.)

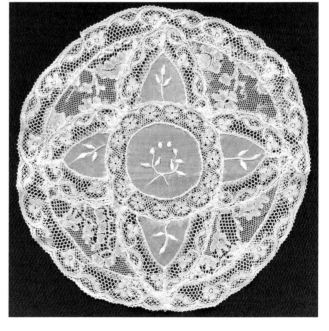

A lace patchwork called Normandy lace is composed of pieces of machine lace. Often very large items are made, such as bedspreads and tablecloths, but this doily is rather smaller, composed of lengths of two different edgings, scraps of a wider machine lace and Schiffli-embroidered voile.

Black needle lace is extremely rare – sewing with black thread is very hard on the eyes. That is not a problem for machines and many black guipures, such as these, were made on Schiffli machines to meet the demand for black lace in the second half of the nineteenth century, when Queen Victoria was in permanent mourning for her husband Prince Albert.

A top-of-the-range example of Schiffli embroidery. There are a number of sections with straightforward embroidery on fine fabric, places where the fabric has been appliquéd to net with curved strips of fabric cut away, plus embroidery on net where the stitches look like tiny pearls. The border and several of the internal areas are chemical lace where unwanted material has been chemically removed. The back is as neat as the front and it is hard to believe that a mat such as this was completed without a considerable amount of very skilled hand-cutting. It is well designed and would have been an expensive small cloth – perhaps an exhibition piece? 45cm × 28cm.

Collection of lace doilies – various techniques including knitting, crochet, filet and bobbin lace, and examples of Leavers and Schiffli machine lace.

CHAPTER 10

SPOT THE
DIFFERENCE

Each of the pages in this chapter has two or more pieces of lace that have similarities but different techniques and/or structures. The challenge is to spot the differences and recognize the techniques.

Two floral discs, each with a background of hexagonal mesh. 8.5cm and 7cm in diameter.

Points to look at

- Mesh: A, on the left, totally regular and beneath other features; B, on the right, slightly irregular merging with other features.
- Outlines: A, buttonhole stitch over a thick thread; B, thick thread goes between the threads of the mesh.
- Petal and leaf filling: A, needle lace stitches; B, cloth stitch and half stitch as in bobbin lace.
- Outer edge: A, surface rings of buttonhole stitch; B, circle of cloth stitch with picots.
- Conclusion: A is needle lace appliquéd to machine net; B is Bucks Point bobbin lace.

Two lace collars which each feature flowers, a scalloped edge and a background of bars with knobbly picots.

In the lower collar each of the flower motifs and scallops are identical, and there is a slightly fuzzy look to the whole. This lace has been worked as a continuous strip and cut and gathered before fitting to a fabric band. The motifs in the other collar are varied; they are arranged nearly, but not quite, symmetrically about the centre web motif (compare the shapes of the flower and leaf sprays to right and left). Some of the flower motifs are three-dimensional with extra petals worked into the base. With magnification (if necessary) it is possible to see the chain stitches that make up the background.

The collar at the top is handmade Irish crochet. The one below is chemical lace, a machine embroidery technique that was developed in 1883, used first for mimicking Irish crochet and now imitating many other laces and creating new designs.

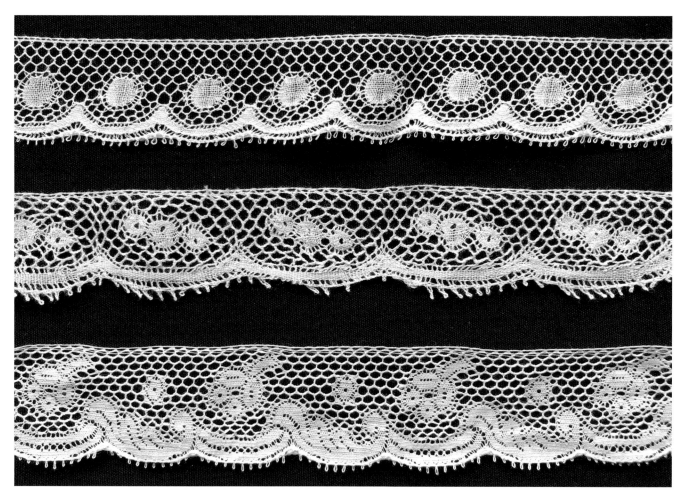

Three lengths of narrow Valenciennes lace from the second half of the nineteenth century (2cm–2.5cm wide). One is bobbin lace; the others are machine made.

The machine lace at the bottom of the picture is totally regular, every repeat is the same and threads in the cloth stitch motifs are tightly packed. In the centre edging no two repeats are exactly the same, the threads curve within the motif and cross each other with a fairly even weave – this is handmade bobbin lace. The picots also differ: in the machine lace they are formed from a single thread, while the hand-made ones are twisted pairs. The third distinctive feature is the ground: in the handmade lace this is irregular with four sides to the mesh which in some places is square, in other areas diamond shaped; the mesh of the machine lace is more rounded and totally regular, with six sides to each mesh. Under magnification it would be possible to see the individual threads of the plaits along the sides of the handmade mesh while in the machine lace, the thread routes are unclear and the sides of the mesh often appear muddled.

Identifying the lace at the top is trickier: the regular weaving of the spots makes it appear to be handmade, but closer inspection of the cloth stitch towards the headside shows the threads in one direction are tightly packed compared with those that cross them, while the picots are single threads and the mesh is hexagonal and totally regular – all features that indicate the lace is machine made.

Magnification of the grounds would confirm the identification, but the other features allow identification without this being necessary.

Four lace edgings from Mrs Tapper's box, each approximately 1.5cm wide. Two are handmade, two are machine; which is which? And which techniques were used in the making?

Parts of the top two laces appear to be woven, which indicates either bobbin lace or lace made on a Barmen machine. Threads in Barmen lace tend to be packed fairly tightly so the lace rarely distorts, and being a machine lace the repeats are totally regular. Bobbin lace, worked by hand and perhaps by an inexperienced lacemaker, or one working at speed, is often irregular and is rarely firm enough to avoid distortion. From this it is clear that the second edging is bobbin lace – it is Torchon lace with cloth-stitch fans and Torchon ground.

The top edging is lace made on a Barmen machine, but with a very odd tufted footside. One end of the lace (lower picture) gives a clue to the origin of the tufts: it appears that the edging started life as two pieces and the tufts and the solid footside are all that remain of a wider machine-made lace.

The third lace is slightly irregular and stitches can be seen to be looped chains. This is a handmade crochet edging, worked with a hook.

In contrast the fourth lace is totally regular, every repeat the same: an example of Schiffli embroidered lace that does not try too hard to imitate a specific handmade lace.

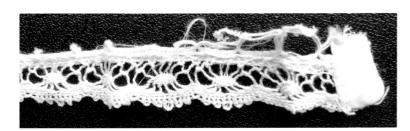

Detail of one end of the first edging.

Three fairly chunky borders for household linen, between 6 and 7cm in width.

The border in the centre has the simple arrangement of filled and open squares typical of filet crochet, lightened towards the top with a row of more open stitches.

The lower border is also crochet, but includes some of the 'novelty braid' described in Chapter 7. In this example there are two lengths of the braid (composed of short lengths of cords linking open squares) while along the inner curve is a straight tape with looped edges.

The texture of the top border is rather strange. It has been photographed in its relaxed state, but stretch it sideways and it changes from a 6cm wide border to one that is nearer 8cm; there is then an obvious looped structure that indicates it is knitted.

Three craft lace doilies; one is knitted, one netted, one Armenian.

It is fairly easy to recognize the hand-knitted doily with its looped stitches forming the six petals, and the irregular mesh of single threads. The two other doilies are harder to identify. Both have a netted structure with different sizes of mesh, and loops of mesh gathered into groups. However, it is only the one on the right that is standard knotted netting worked with a shuttle. The doily on the left is Armenian, a knotted needle lace worked with a needle. There is a slightly different 'look' given by the two techniques, which becomes more obvious the more examples you see. There is also a slight difference in the knots when seen under magnification.

Knitting 13cm diameter, Armenian 21cm, netting 25cm.

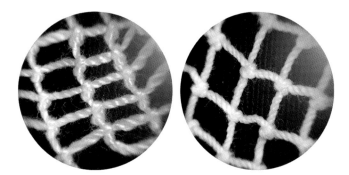

Detail of the knots. On the left are the needle-made knots of the Armenian lace, which are to one side of the crossings. On the right are the netted knots, which fit squarely across the thread junctions.

Two small jabots, both approximately 20cm long, both composed of two layers of lace. One is quite chunky, the other is more delicate, so they would be appropriate for different styles of dress.

The jabot on the left has a background of chain loops while closely packed stitches make up simple stylized flowers and leaves which are typical of Irish crochet. An additional feature is the bunch of crocheted pompoms.

The flowers and leaves of the second jabot are far more realistic. Two different techniques have been used – needle and bobbin lace. The tear-drop shape in the centre, with a single flower, including a raised petal, is needle lace with the deli-

cate Point de Gaze ground, while the other flowers, the big leaf at the point and all the connecting features are bobbin lace. So this is the mixed lace known as Brussels Duchesse. When the Point de Gaze panel is viewed from the back it is possible to see the stitching that holds the raised petal in place and the needle lace ground to the bobbin lace outline. The jabot has been made in two pieces and loosely linked at the narrow point.

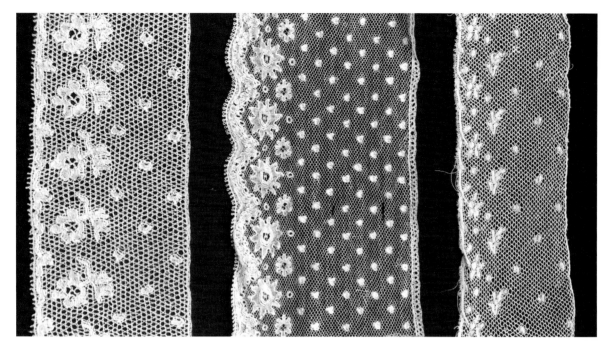

Short lengths of three borders, all with mesh ground; headsides are on the left. 5.5cm–8cm wide.

In the first border, the ground is clearly kat stitch. Grounds in the other two pieces appear to be hexagonal, and magnification confirms this showing that the mesh is also handmade bobbin lace. This is surprising when you look at the headsides. The headside on the right-hand border is frayed, which you would expect to see in machine lace cut from a wider piece, and there is little sign of picots. The middle piece does have picots, but these are clearly a machine-made strip with single thread loops. It is only the border on the left that shows normal bobbin-lace picots of twisted pairs, with the threads coming out then back into the lace.

The border on the right is Valenciennes in style, with no outlining threads, while the other two laces have gimps finished with cut ends after each little motif, indicating the lace is not machine made.

The frayed edge on the border on the right is presumably the result of wear and tear, but it is unclear why the machine picots have been added to the centre piece. However, everything apart from the picots points to all three borders being handmade bobbin lace.

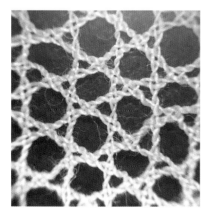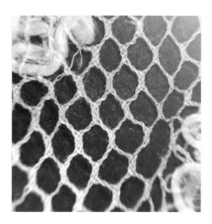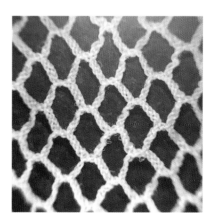

The style of the grounds (shown here in the same order as the lace) leads to the conclusion that these borders are, from left to right: Bucks Point with kat stitch ground; Mechlin; Valenciennes.

Four small doilies, all between 14cm and 15cm in diameter.

The bright white doily, lower left, has a label telling us it was made in India. Washing symbols were standardized in 1966, which indicates this doily was bought after that date. The doily is crochet, started in the middle with mainly closely worked stitches and spaces on later rounds; these are the stitches used in filet crochet.

The three other doilies are early twentieth century, all from sets that include larger versions. The doily top right is certainly bobbin lace – a common combination of scallops, leaf-shaped tallies, plaits and half-stitch diamonds. Lace like this is still made in China, but was previously produced in many lace-making areas, and is often described as Cluny.

The doily bottom right is more of a puzzle. The border could certainly be worked with bobbins, but the clothwork in the central panel is too tightly packed to be bobbin lace, also it is unlikely that bobbin lace would be cut in this way, all of which indicates that the centre is machine made. As it is also unlikely that bobbin lace would be put round a panel where the lace has been cut to shape, the conclusion is the border is also machine made, both made on a Barmen machine.

The doily top left is also machine made; in this case it is a complex piece of Schiffli embroidery with a net background, fabric flowers and leaves, and small areas of open stitching.

Three pieces of lace, all with a square mesh and the pattern created by filling selected squares while leaving the rest of the mesh empty.

The filet crochet 'LACE' panel has the largest mesh. Each side of each square is a bar of looped stitches, on the horizontal the bar is a short chain of two stitches, on the verticals it is a stitch known as a treble – chain and treble can look very alike. The spaces are filled as the lace is made by working two trebles instead of the two chain stitches.

The oldest technique is the filet doily (15cm across). The background is a handmade square mesh, with a knot in each corner. The design of flowers and leaves has been added with a simple darning stitch.

The smallest of the meshes was machine made on a curtain-net machine, which produces a square mesh with no knots or looping, and at the same time weaves in the closely filled design. (The two square panels were woven as part of a wide fabric, designed to be cut up and used as separate pieces.)

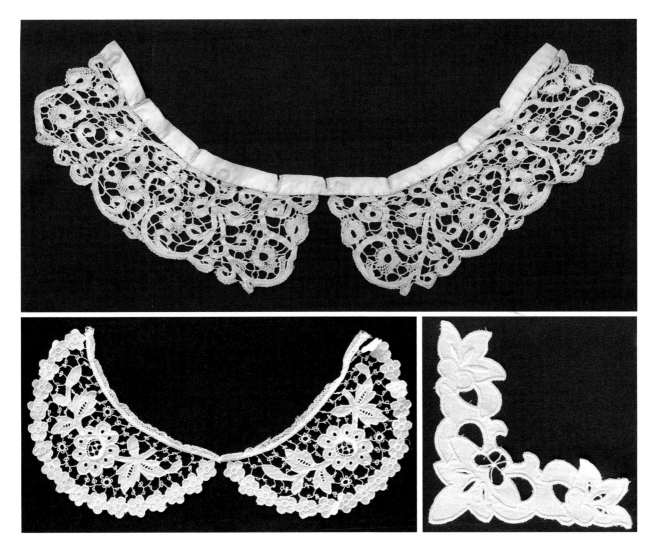

Two collars and the corner of a cloth. Are these all lace?

The little Peter Pan collar (7cm wide) with its large central flowers and leaves, and border of five-petal flowers, is an extremely good copy of a Carrickmacross guipure (see Chapter 7). The outlines, bars, little rings and picots have all been machine embroidered, as has the raised area in the centre of the flower. Unwanted fabric would be difficult to cut from behind machine embroidered bars so would have been chemically treated to be dissolved away.

The L-shaped corner (14cm along the sides) is also embroidered, in this case hand embroidery on cotton fabric. The outlines are closely worked buttonhole stitch, small areas have been cut out and a tiny amount of decorative stitching worked. This type of embroidery is usually described as Richelieu work and cannot really be described as lace,

although it is closely related to other whitework such as Broderie Anglaise. It is another reminder of the difficulty in defining boundaries when looking at lace and related crafts.

What about the collar at the top? Is that also fabric based? It certainly has some similarities to the other pieces on this page, and the inner edge is definitely fabric (with notches to allow it to be tucked inside a neckline) but what about the rest? Look at it more closely and you can see the elements of Cantu bobbin lace: cloth-stitch stems with curly spurs and three-petal flowers all linked by bars of plaited pairs (see Chapter 5).

Where to start with this group of four discs, ranging in size from 4cm to 10cm in diameter?

Do you think any are machine made? Are there techniques that you recognize? Which ones have bunches of threads in the centre? Or bunches of loops towards the outer border?

Hairpin crochet requires loops to be collected into groups – that is the technique used for the doily top right. The foundation spokes for Tenerife require multiple threads to go across the centre. This has formed the bunching in the centre of a single Tenerife wheel, top left.

The two other disks have open centres. The one on the left is needle lace – with closely worked buttonhole stitch creating bars, picots and little triangles. The tiny piece is tatting formed entirely of the double stitch which is structurally a buttonhole stitch followed by a reverse buttonhole stitch.

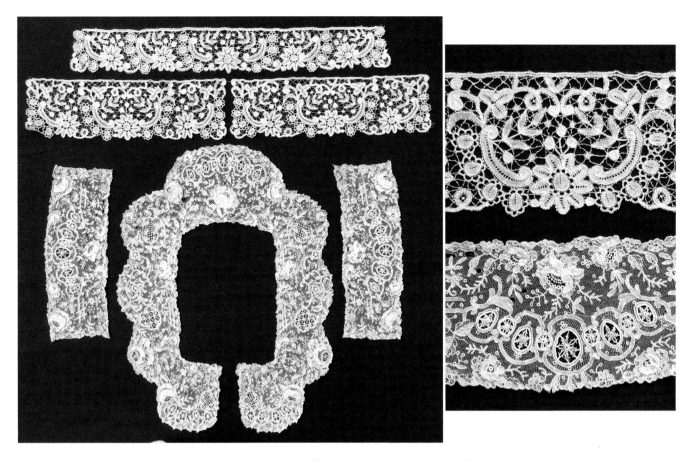

Two late nineteenth-century collar and cuff sets, showing very different collar shapes but similar cuffs. On the right are sections from the centre of the cuffs that show two approaches to creating lace with floral motifs.

The straight collar at the top is 40cm long and would have been worn flat around the high neck of a formal long-sleeved blouse, with the lace cuffs stitched to the surface of a deep-buttoned cuff. The shape of the cuffs with the curved collar suggest that these were also intended for a blouse with closely fitting cuffs and a high neck, in this case the collar would sit on the shoulders below the neckline.

Both sets are handmade lace; both are pieced laces and both feature flower, leaf and scroll motifs. One set is needle lace, the other is bobbin. Which is which?

Looking at the images on the right you can see that the lower cuff has a variety of naturalistic flowers including the roses with raised petals that are found in Point de Gaze needle lace, it also has the typical light mesh ground of twisted buttonhole stitch. In contrast the flowers in the cuff at the top are more stylized, linked by bars with picots and there is no mesh ground. This is the bobbin lace known as Bruges Duchesse.

MARCH. 1876.

THE NEWEST FRENCH FASHIONS,
DESIGNED FOR
"THE LADIES' TREASURY."

A hand-coloured fashion plate from a bound collection of the 1876 issues of *The Ladies' Treasury*, a monthly magazine for middle-class ladies. Many yards of lace were needed for these ensembles, but most of the flounces, sleeve ruffles and so on could be recycled when fashions changed. More difficult to re-use are the shaped pieces such as the back panel and collars, which is why so many collars have survived, of all shapes and sizes and every type of lace.

CHAPTER 11

BUT WHAT IS IT FOR?

Looked at from one angle lace is of absolutely no use, but there is a lot of it about, some nearly 500 years old, so it must have some value. Lace is, and was, primarily for ornament, and it may also show status. In the past the making of lace by hand was a way to supplement the family income, for today's lacemaker it offers a variety of fascinating and challenging crafts. The development of machine lace through the nineteenth century was a key driver of the Industrial Revolution and an early adopter of punch-card technology (the forerunner of computing). Continuing innovation can be seen today on the high street and catwalks.

One lace that does have a practical use is a window curtain, particularly where windows or glazed doors are close to the pavement – lace will let in the light while keeping out the stares of passers-by and softening the impact of strong sunshine or unattractive views. The curtain for the lower half of a window is known as a *brise-bise*; these are often worked in filet crochet or are fabric with a lace border. However, the vast majority of lace curtains are machine lace, usually today worked in synthetic thread, and many is the lace curtain that has ended up in the dressing-up box, or amateur theatre wardrobe, to dress a princess, fairy or bride.

Curtain on a street door in Matera, Italy. This is machine lace but is a design that could easily be reproduced in filet or filet crochet (2019).

Household Linen

Household linen is the catch-all name given to all the fabric items such as sheets, pillow cases, table cloths and so on that are regularly used in the home. Originally most of these items were made from linen fabric – hence the name – today cotton and synthetic threads are more likely. From the sixteenth century onwards lace has been used to trim these items, usually as edgings, but occasionally as an insertion to join two widths of hand-woven linen and sometimes as a complete item. In the Victorian period lace could be found on almost everything within the home, the lace either handmade, or increasingly using the great variety of tape and machine laces. As the twentieth century progressed the use of lace in the home gradually decreased, but has never completely disappeared.

Filet crochet edging on a hand-embroidered pillow case, a wedding present for Jean and David from a family friend (1960s).

Terylene is one of the early synthetic yarns developed in 1941 and extensively used for curtains and other household items, such as this tablecloth, which was advertised in a 1976 issue of *Woman and Home*. A tablecloth of this type would have been made on a Leavers or curtain machine.

Cluny bobbin lace doilies in three sizes (12.5cm, 20cm, 34cm). These doilies appear to be part of a set: all have the same circle of cloth-stitch panels alternating with half stitch with a surface tally but there are slight variations in the ways the circles are worked that indicate they have come from different workshops. Doilies like these, made in cotton, usually launder well.

This is a typical example of a Leavers lace table cloth, worked in two colours of cotton. This one is a square (130cm × 130cm) with a design that works well on a circular table. The cloth has survived considerable usage since purchase, probably in the 1950s, but possibly earlier.

An impressive piece of Maltese bobbin lace. It appears to be a mat (50cm × 66cm) but was possibly intended as a decorative panel. It is a high-quality piece with the Maltese crosses indicating it was made on the island of Malta. An unusual feature is the insert with the letter 'V'. The letter and its background mesh appear to have been made at a different time by a different hand. Was the mat exported with an empty panel that could be used to record a person or event?

Maintaining church linens, especially those with lace borders, is a skilled and demanding task, but some churches still retain the tradition of lace on vestments, altar cloths and smaller items. Someone in this English village church has taken great care with the arrangement of this altar cloth and its filet crochet border.

Filet crochet is popular in Italian churches where there are also some beautiful machine-made laces on the altars and occasionally some impressive modern needle lace (not always easy to photograph).

Crochet curtain for one of the boat's portholes.
Courtesy Harold and Katey Bond.

Crochet was popular with women who lived and worked on the canal boats. It was easy to work, to put down and pick up when other tasks allowed, and the finished lace could be boil-washed to deal with the inevitable dirt on boats that transported coal and other industrial materials. The traditional furnishings in this cabin interior, including the white crochet pelmet and borders for the curtains that close off the engine area, have been researched and made by Katey Bond. The cushions and blankets are also crochet, the latter composed of 'granny squares' worked in wool. Courtesy Harold and Katy Bond.

Small items such as this lavender bag are often projects for beginner lacemakers to practice turning corners and joining start to finish. This example (8cm across) has a Torchon edging.

Patterns for both fashion and household items are included in this large insert from an 1874 issue of *The Young Ladies' Journal*. There is a ruffle and a fichu of imitation Honiton; a dress trimming of Medieval Lace and two other patterns for Medieval Lace which look rather heavy for dresses but would have been ideal to edge a curtain or antimacassar, or perhaps the edging on a shelf in a china cabinet or as a pelmet on a mantelpiece. There is also a pattern for a round cushion in Point Lace. These three types of tape lace are distinctly different and would have been recognized as such by the young ladies of the period, and their mothers.

It would be rare to find a netting pattern in a twentieth-century magazine, but they were common in the Victorian period. This is a piano stool *couvette* (cover), described in *The Ladies' Treasury* in 1876, which required three mesh sticks – 3/8 in, 1/2in, 5/8 in – for making the net, plus a rug needle for darning in the detail. Instructions are minimal, starting with, 'The foundation is 36 loops netted with no1 mesh and drawn up in a small circle'. A disc that started with thirty-six loops should have finished with eighteen points, not nineteen as there are in this illustration – the print would have been prepared by an engraver who may not have been looking at an actual example.

This netted doily has a fabric centre, but is otherwise similar in construction to the couvette. The odd number of points is more obvious since different arrangements of embroidery stitches are used. The origin of this problem would have been the first row which requires dozens of loops, much more difficult to count than the thirty-six loops needed to start the stool cover.

Sachets

Lace-trimmed sachets have been made to store items such as stockings or handkerchiefs, and smaller sachets filled with lavender or other scented materials might be placed inside. One of the early twentieth-century organizations producing these sachets was the Aemilia Ars Society, which was a craft collective established in Bologna, Italy in 1898. Lace was one of the many crafts practised there, often using designs taken from the sixteenth and seventeenth centuries. All items made by the society carried a small trademark button.

From its shape, this rectangular sachet (29cm × 14cm) was probably for stockings. The chemical lace, that is barely visible until backed with coloured paper, has been hand stitched to the fabric that forms the flap, with unwanted fabric cut away from the back. Courtesy Sheila Priestly.

This 27cm square linen sachet carries the trademark Aemelia Ars button. It probably once held underwear (when bought, the silk lining was stuck together with the remains of some kind of cosmetic). Today Aemelia Ars is best known for its needle lace, but both needle and bobbin lace can be seen in this piece. Circular needle lace motifs are set into the front panel; there is a bobbin lace insertion between front and back panels and a bobbin lace edging all the way round. The pattern for the insertion appears to have been taken from *Le Pompe*, a bobbin-lace pattern book first published in Venice in 1557. The Society was wound up in 1930 so this piece can be safely dated to the years between 1898 and 1930.

This 44cm square handkerchief is of Duchesse Application lace (i.e. bobbin lace applied to machine net) made in the second half of the nineteenth century. The border ranges in width from 14 to 19cm and there is so little fabric in the centre that it would be of little use for mopping even the daintiest of a lady's tears.

Handkerchiefs

In Charles Dickens' novel *Oliver Twist* (first published as a serial in 1837) Oliver was accused of stealing a handkerchief – a not uncommon crime at a time when handkerchiefs with wide lace borders were often large and valuable items. These were 'showers' carried by men and women as part of fashionable dress and might be used like a fan at social occasions. By the 1890s much smaller decorative handkerchiefs, described as 'stick up hankies', were worn tucked into the top pocket of a jacket.

By the end of the nineteenth century men's handkerchiefs were usually undecorated and ladies' handkerchiefs were smaller, but still often edged with lace. Many women today still like their hankies with a lace edging, frequently tatting, crochet or bobbin lace made by themselves or a friend or family member.

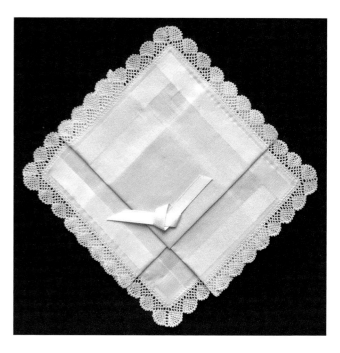

Example of a late twentieth-century cotton handkerchief edged with simple bobbin lace and folded for presentation.

This is one corner of an early nineteenth-century handkerchief, 53cm square with a 4cm wide border of Mechlin bobbin lace, plus a narrow insertion of Valenciennes lace and a posy of white-work flowers. Note that a substantial length of the lace is needed to go round the corner. This is a handkerchief that would have gathered well to tuck in a pocket or wave nonchalantly from a hand.

Handkerchief corner with hand embroidery and crochet edging, one of many handkerchiefs worked by Diane Cooper's grandmother for herself and her family.

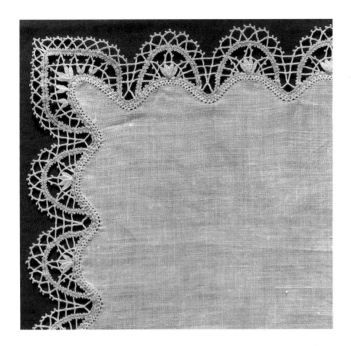

There is a tradition of making a special handkerchief for a bride often featuring hearts, flowers or other appropriate motifs. This scalloped border of Bedfordshire bobbin lace is an example of a traditional fertility pattern.

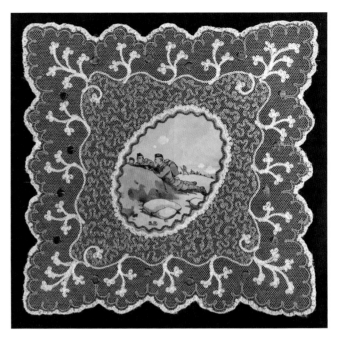

Numerous souvenir handkerchiefs with lace borders have survived, the majority brought from France and many, particularly those with a silk centre, are in a poor state. This one is rather different and should perhaps be called a souvenir panel rather than a handkerchief. The main technique is tambour on net, with some needle-running and the addition of a few sequins. The soldiers and the 'SR' in the printed oval suggest that it might have been made for members of the Scottish Rifles to give to their families.

Bonnets

Until well into the twentieth century, women and girls were expected to have their heads covered when they went out and often also within the home. Many of the head coverings can be described as bonnets. Fabric bonnets, often with a lace trim, were worn by women at all levels of society, and were part of traditional dress in many parts of Europe. Bonnets made of plaited straw, or other stiff materials were usually decorated with lace, ribbons, feathers and/or flowers. A bonnet veil (as described in Chapter 7) might be attached above the brim and often there was a frill of lace within the brim to frame the face.

With two folds and a few stitches the wedding handkerchief can be converted into a bonnet for a baby's christening. This example, also Bedfordshire, has two decorative corners and a narrow edging.

This is an adult-size bonnet of a style often worn by babies: cotton fabric with frills of machine-made Valenciennes lace. As with babies' bonnets there is a drawstring at the back to shape the bonnet to the head.

It was not easy to recognize this as a bonnet until it was put on a head; it looked more like a badly shaped bowl. The fabric is a simple damask (possibly once part of a tablecloth) and the 6cm wide border is crochet lace.

A pretty bonnet assembled from crochet motifs – half have a central circle and the others have central flowers with raised petals – plus a scalloped border, finished with a pink ribbon.

An elaborate bonnet composed of layers of handmade Valenciennes lace and Broderie Anglaise. This would have been an expensive item and one that required very skilled laundering.

This is not exactly a bonnet, but a head-covering known as a 'boudoir cap', worn by a lady within her boudoir (bedroom/dressing area) before her hair had been dressed for the day. 1920s.

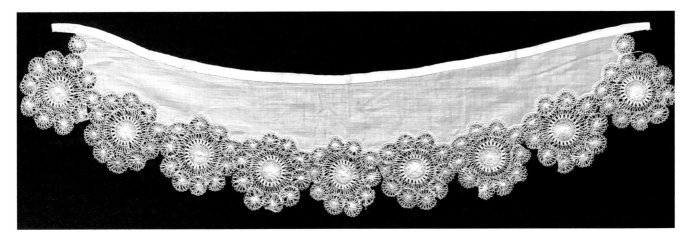

Our first thought was that this length of fine linen edged with Tenerife wheels is a collar. It is long enough but when tried around shoulders or neck it doesn't sit right. The folded tape on the edge is hollow so could take a gathering thread, but that still wouldn't work as a collar. Could it be the pelmet/edging on a shelf in a china cabinet? Probably not, as there is a slight curve to the piece and the fabric is so fine that it is almost certainly clothing, not furnishings. The answer only came when the panel was held around a head – it is just the right shape for lining the brim of a bonnet.

a   b   c   d

a. Mid-nineteenth century Maltese lappets. These are relatively heavy in construction, which would have gone well with the large jackets and crinoline skirts of the period. They were probably worn under a small bonnet or hat. **b.** Chantilly tie featuring decorative ends of half-stitch petals and leaves, surrounded by thick gimps. The background is point ground and there are small areas of honeycomb fillings. A shaped piece such as this requires threads to be added as the shape widens and taken out as the work narrows. **c.** Lappets are usually bobbin or needle lace so it took a while to realize that this long length (160cm × 9cm) of machine-made lace was a finished item. The scalloped edges, curved ends and open spaces have been carefully cut from a wide lace fabric made on a Leavers machine. Short lengths of machine-made picots have been stitched around each end, while picots along the sides are part of the original fabric. It seems likely that this was intended as something like a bow for the back of a wedding dress, not as a lappet. **d.** This long piece of a very simple Maltese lace was acquired many years ago and we are still unsure of its purpose. It is a simple design and came with two other identical pieces. Obviously not high fashion, but was this once part of a cap worn by an Edwardian housemaid?

Lappets and Ties

Long streamers of lace, known as lappets, were part of a lady's headwear from the seventeenth to the nineteenth centuries. Early examples were often part of a set with a headpiece also of lace. Fashions changed over the years, as did the etiquette of how lappets should be worn. By the middle of Victoria's reign lappets had become less elaborate and were often just simple ties that might be worn around the neck or used to hold a bonnet in place. Four very different examples of lappets are shown opposite.

Wearing lappets could be tricky: in 1876 the fashion pages of *The Ladies' Treasury* recorded that 'at the opening of parliament the Queen [Victoria] wore on her head a small pointed cap having at the back very long lappets, upon the cap a small crown of diamonds. As her majesty took her seat on the throne she unfortunately sat on the ends of the lappets which pulled the crown nearly off her head.'

Other Head Coverings

Some Jewish traditions require women to have a head covering which might be a small lace cap, while all women entering a mosque must have their heads covered. The simplest covering is a headscarf and in Muslim countries, such as Turkey, the scarves are often finished with a lace trim known as an oya. Muslim men wear a closely fitting cap known as a kufi for prayers – kufis are often knitted or crocheted with a lacy pattern.

In Spain and other Catholic countries, women attending church and other formal occasions have been expected to wear a lace mantilla or other head covering. The traditional colour for a mantilla is black with white worn by unmarried girls and for special occasions such as weddings. Mantillas and other veils may be passed down through the generations for use at weddings, first communions and other important events.

Oya trims may be machine made but are more often crochet or, as here, Armenian needle lace. This example was bought in Turkey in 1993. Similar flowers are made in Greece, which is one of the countries where the lace is known as Bebilla (or Bibilla). Petals are about 1.5cm long.

In this Spanish postcard the wearing of a mantilla is illustrated using a piece of machine-made lace (the card came with an envelope to protect the lace in the post). Courtesy Elaine Williams.

Lace for Men

Until the eighteenth century lace was as popular for men as for women, but from 1800 onwards men have rarely worn lace except for ceremonial occasions. A lace jabot, sometimes with matching cuffs, may be part of official dress for roles such as sheriff, mayor or university chancellor. Often these are of machine made lace but many have been made by local lacemakers.

Bucks Point jabot made by Gil in 2000 for her husband when he was pro-vice chancellor of Newcastle University. The lace features a lion passant and St Cuthbert's cross, both motifs taken from the university's coat of arms. 21.5cm deep.

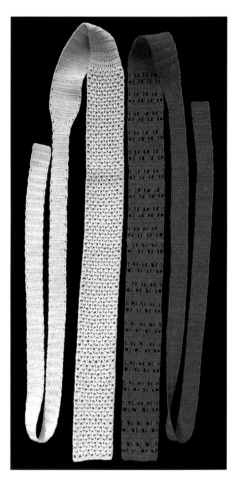

For a short while in the 1960s men's fashion included crochet ties; these 4cm wide examples were made by Jean for her husband.

Underwear

From the time lace was first made in the sixteenth century, lace has trimmed underwear. The elaborate ruffs and cuffs we see on Elizabethan portraits actually had their origins in narrow lace trims on the gathered cuffs and necklines of sixteenth-century smocks and shirts. As the lace got wider and more elaborate it needed special laundering and became a separate item.

The smock/shirt served as both undergarment and sleepwear, but over time these roles have become separated: shirt and nightshirt for men (rarely lace trimmed); petticoat and nightgown for women (frequently with lace). At any time in the past 200 years it is likely that a high proportion of women would have had at least a narrow lace trim on some or all of their underwear.

A camisole is a short garment that at times would have been worn under a corset and at other times over it as a short petticoat. This example with its Torchon trim and straps is early twentieth century.

Ankle-length, long-sleeved nightgowns trimmed with lace were popular with Queen Victoria and there are several of her gowns with Valenciennes lace in collections around the world. This gown of a similar style was made rather later, probably early in the twentieth century, ending up in a charity shop some seventy years later. It has a 16cm wide lace collar, lace cuffs and numerous insertions and frills, all of Torchon bobbin lace.

Corsets may also include lace. At the end of the nineteenth century the lace would have been a trim.

SWANBILL CORSETS. (Regd.)
Medium, 17/6 ; Tall, 18/6 ; Short, 14/6.

SWANBILL CORSET. (Regd.)
Price 21/-

SWANBILL BELT CORSET. (Regd.)
Price 21/- and 31/6.

SWANBILL BELT. (Regd.)
Price 21/-

ADDLEY BOURNE,
LADIES' WAREHOUSE,
37, PICCADILLY (Opposite St. James's Church), LONDON,
AND AT PARIS.

The corsets in this 1976 advert have lace panels worked in synthetic thread that would have assisted in providing support.

A garment like this may be called a 'bust flattener' as it has very little in the way of shaping. The depth is 34cm and overall length is 72cm, fastened at the back with large press-studs. It was made on a Pusher machine and the large holes towards the top and bottom are there to take ribbons.

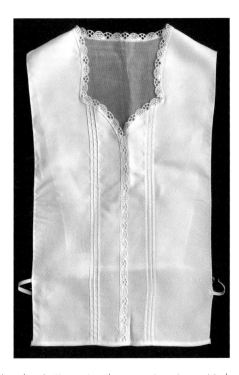

This is a chemisette, part undergarment, part meant to be seen. Basically it is a blouse without sleeves or sides that is worn under another garment to show a lace collar at the neckline. (A chemise is rather different; it is an undergarment that we might now call a petticoat.) 44cm × 17cm. Courtesy Sheila Priestly.

The lace insertion in a bra bought in 2019 was definitely made on a Raschel machine with polyester thread, and it is likely that the 1976 corsets used the same type of lace. (Corsets went out of general use in the 1980s, but teenage granddaughters tell us they are coming back into fashion.)

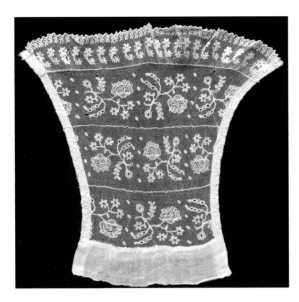

The smaller, rectangular panel (20cm × 15cm) is two lengths of Schiffli-embroidered whitework on either side of a length of pleated fabric; at the top is an edging of machine-made Valenciennes. Both panels are bound at the sides with soft fabric.

An alternative to a chemisette was a modesty panel, which was worn pinned or stitched inside the neckline of a blouse or dress. The two panels here were in Mrs Tapper's box so probably assembled by her in the early 1900s to fit the necklines of specific garments. The shaped panel is composed of lengths of needle-run net. 21cm × 21cm

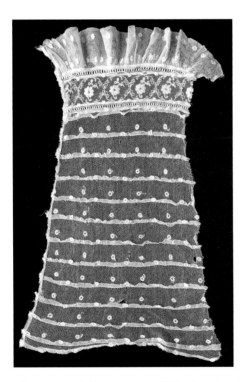

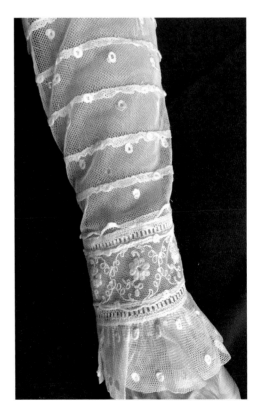

What was the purpose of this strange panel? The first thought was a modesty vest, but it is the wrong shape. Turn it round and fit it around a wrist and the answer becomes clear – it is a sleeve that has been cut along the seam.

Most of the sleeve is composed of cotton bobbinet with surface decoration of couched threads applied with a Cornely sewing machine. The wrist band is decorated with flowers and tendrils, while the rest of the net has regularly arranged small circles. The net is used double for the wrist frill while small pleats give interest to the main body of the sleeve. Two machine-made tapes connect the three sections at the wrist.

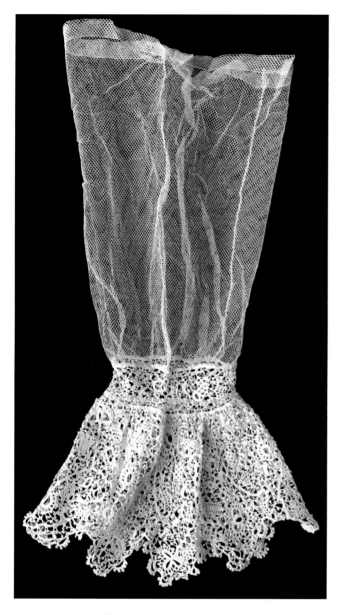

Under-sleeves with lace cuffs were worn during the nineteenth century and occasionally in the twentieth. This single sleeve was the only piece of its kind in Mrs Tapper's box. The sleeve is plain net with a hem that would have been loosely stitched to the inside of an outer sleeve. The cuff/ruffle is Irish crochet.

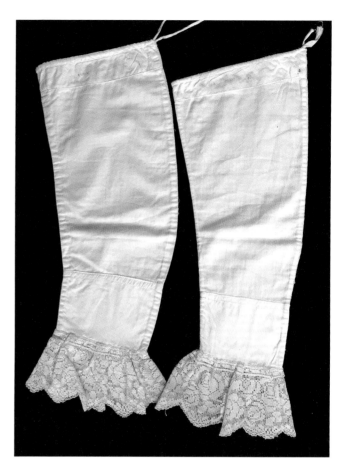

This is a more substantial pair of under-sleeves finished with a filet crochet cuff. They have drawstrings at the top, which presumably tied round the upper arm (and were probably not particularly comfortable).

Collars and Cuffs

Collars and cuffs often come in sets, and most are designed to be detachable, easily removed for laundering. Some have a straight footside intended to be stitched to the edge of a garment, in others the footside is more decorative. Cuffs with this type of edge are attached to the surface of a sleeve with a few stitches, collars may need to be stitched, but in some cases they will just lie over the shoulders.

An early twentieth-century collar and cuff set which still has its shop label. It has been assembled by a professional seamstress from cotton tape and two different machine-made laces. It would have been left to the purchaser to separate the cuffs and neaten the tape ends. Collar 5cm wide, 22cm long.

For this collar and sleeve ruffle set three pieces appear to have been cut from a single length (6cm wide) of Bucks Point with a kat stitch ground. There are two 80cm long pieces, one still joined as it would have been as a sleeve ruffle (upper left). Below the ruffle is a third length, 33cm long, which has been backed with a length of patterned machine net (see image on the right with coloured paper between the net and lace) and then given hooks and eyes to make a standing collar. (Probably mid-nineteenth century.)

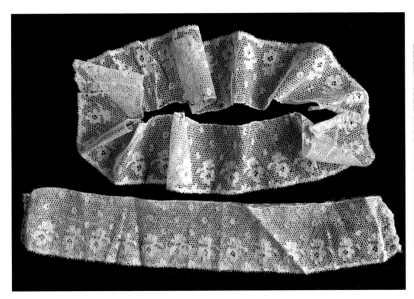

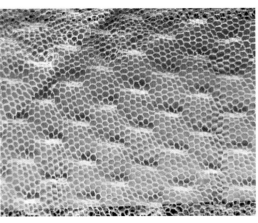

This is an example of a late nineteenth-century chemical lace collar (machine embroidered on net) that sits neatly around the neck and shoulders and would need little if any stitching to keep it in position.

This small triangle of Pusher lace with needle-run outlines could be described as a veil or fichu; it might be worn over the hair or around the neck and shoulders. (Note the piece of machine-made picot strip that has become detached at the left-hand corner.) Short sides of the triangle are 68cm.

A more elaborate fichu or cape. This is also needle-run on Pusher lace and it is carefully shaped so it lies neatly in two layers across the shoulders.

Weddings

There are plenty of places where lace may be found at a traditional-style wedding, the most obvious being the bride's dress and veil. Other possibilities are lace flowers for buttonholes, table and cake decoration and even complete bouquets, also cake bands, garters, ring cushions, coronets for the bride and headbands for the bridesmaids, handkerchiefs for the mothers…

Torchon garter worked with a gap to take elastic and ribbon – the latter providing the blue for the traditional requirement for a bride that she should wear 'something old, something new, something borrowed, something blue'.

Bridal coronet of Bruges Flower lace stiffened with sugar.

Accessories

Gloves, fans, parasols and bags are among the many accessories where lace might be found, either as decoration or forming the whole item. Lace is second only to paper in popularity as a material for fan leaves, and if you look far enough you will find virtually every type of lace, from delicate eighteenth-century bobbin lace to colourful modern designs using mixed techniques, but the fans you are most likely to find today are ones made for the tourist market. There are two main types of tourist fans: ones with plastic fan-sticks and black or brightly coloured machine-lace leaf, and ones with wood or plastic sticks and a leaf of Battenberg tape lace. Battenberg tape parasols, both full size and miniature are also readily available, mostly made in China (see Chapter 7).

Parasols were once considered essential to protect a lady's complexion from the sun and as they were part of fashionable outfits in the eighteenth and nineteenth centuries, they often included lace. This large parasol with a covering of black machine-made Chantilly was part of Therese Bates' collection.

Tourist fan bought in Spain: plastic sticks and a paper fan-leaf edged with a band of black machine-made lace.

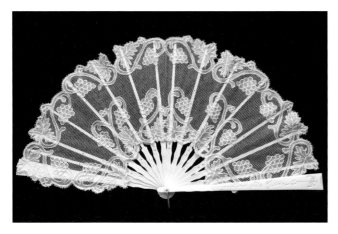

Twenty-first century Carrickmacross fan with nineteenth century sticks.

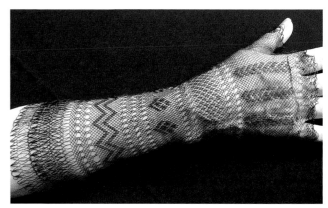

Black netted mittens were worn during the Victorian period for both day and evening wear. This example has an elaborate pattern created by using different sizes of mesh stick and bringing together groups of loops – it would not have been an easy item to make.

Baby and Children's Clothes

For centuries nursemaids and mothers were kept busy maintaining the mass of lace worn by their babies and toddlers. In the 1800s babies, like adults, wore many layers of clothes starting next to the skin with a fine cotton or linen shirt. These shirts were cut from a single strip of fabric around 25cm deep and 60cm long; sometimes this is the full width of the linen so there is a selvage on both front edges. There are usually small capped sleeves and clever underarm gussets (the only added fabric). Most of the dozen or more shirts we have been given are beautifully stitched and many are trimmed with narrow lace, usually machine-made Valenciennes, occasionally handmade bobbin lace.

A padded corset was worn over the shirt with the shirt flaps turned down and pinned in place (ordinary pins, not safety ones!). Over the corset was a petticoat and over the petticoat was a long dress, often trimmed with lace. Many of these long dresses have survived, treasured in families as christening gowns (but now rarely worn as babies today are seldom christened, and are usually too big for a nineteenth-century gown).

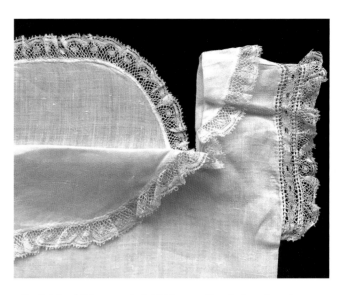

The fabric of this up-market shirt is exceptionally fine; there is more lace than usual (in this case it is handmade) and the flaps have been cut to provide an extra cap to the sleeve. On the other hand there is no underarm gusset so this may not have been as comfortable for the baby.

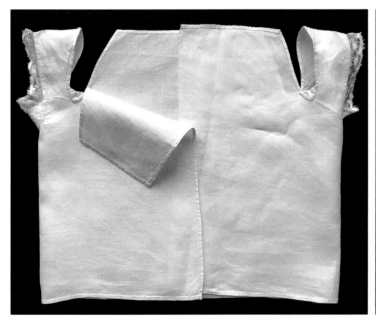

A standard linen shirt with the small sleeves, front opening with no fastening, and flaps that fold down over the corset at front and back. A detail of the underarm gusset (a triangle of fabric) can be seen on the right, which also shows how the fold point has been strengthened in a garment that would see many years of use with a number of wriggling babies. The lace on the sleeve is machine-made Valenciennes (1.5cm wide).

It was considered important for a baby's head to be covered at all times, sometimes with two bonnets – one plain, worn day and night, one fancy to go over the top for warmth or show. This is a small bonnet of Ayrshire whitework that was probably everyday wear for a baby in a middle-class family. These bonnets usually have several channels threaded with narrow cords that can be pulled up to fit the bonnet to a small baby's head, and released as the baby grows. The circular panel at the back of the bonnet is just 6cm across.

Detail of the edging and two insertions around the skirt of the gown.

This nineteenth-century baby's gown was rescued in a filthy state from a rug stall at an antiques fair. It took many washes to reveal that it was entirely handmade, including the perfect pin-tucks, the whitework embroidery on the bodice and the numerous lengths of Bucks Point edgings and insertions. It is an exceptionally long gown: 99cm from waist to hem and 8.5cm from waist to neck. A narrow lace edges the sleeves and there is a wider edging at the bottom of the gown. Five short lengths of a narrow insertion are used to form the front of the bodice. Gowns of this type changed little over many decades so are difficult to date. From the quality of workmanship this one probably comes from the middle of the nineteenth century.

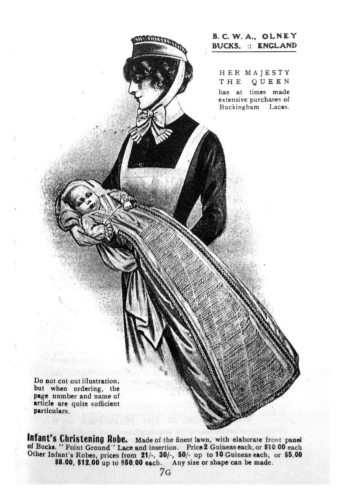

Long gowns were among the items sold through the Bucks Cottage
Workers Association at the beginning of the twentieth century.
This one is described as having an elaborate front panel of 'Point
Ground' lace and insertions. In this context 'lace' would have meant
the scalloped edging along the sides of the panel, and 'insertions'
the straight pieces across the panel. There was obviously a market
in America for these gowns as the price is given in dollars as well
as pounds. (The catalogue was posted to potential customers who
returned it with their order.)

This little girl's dress from the 1940s is simple in style and would have
been worn with a petticoat. The bodice and sleeves of the dress are
plain net, the skirt fabric is embroidered by a Cornely machine. 40cm
from hem to neck.

Detail of the embroidery on the skirt.

As babies became more active both boys and girls went into short dresses, these often embroidered and trimmed with lace – small boys in dresses can be seen in photos taken well into the 1920s. In the 1960s there was a sharp decline in the use of lace on even girls' clothing as easy-care fabrics came on to the market and stretchy sleep-suits took the place of lace-trimmed night gowns. Lace can again be found on clothing for small girls, but today it is likely to be machine lace as part of the structure of the garment, not just as a trim.

Today we would probably assume that this is a girl's dress, but even as late as 1920 small boys might be put into dresses for photographs and special occasions.

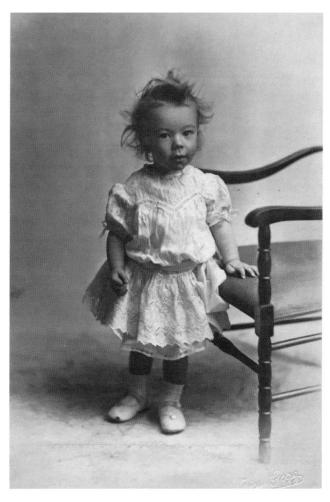

A studio portrait of Gil's father probably taken in 1918 when he was two years old.

Detail of front panel of dress.

An arrangement of small bobbin and needle lace flowers.

CHAPTER 12

ODDS AND ENDS

Throughout the past five centuries lace has been mainly for fashion and furnishings, but there are many other ways in which lace techniques have been used, anything from stents to repair arteries to large-scale architectural installations. Here are some of the smaller items you might find.

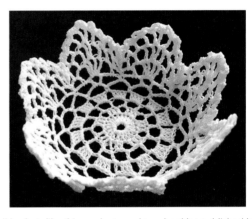

Small baskets like this can be traced to a booklet published by the thread manufacturer Twilleys in the 1960s. This was one of many pattern books and booklets published in that decade for everything from complete dresses to ornaments. The basket has been stiffened with sugar, and has neither softened nor discoloured in more than five decades. 11cms across, 3.5cm deep.

Once essential for any table, weighted jug covers are today relatively rare, but this crochet example (16cm diameter) is in regular use.
Courtesy Margaret Sutcliffe.

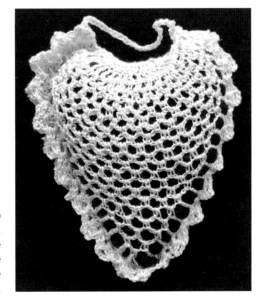

Pins were essential when most women were expected to make clothes and do running repairs for their families. Pins are easier to manage if kept in a pin cushion. This is a utilitarian example with a crocheted pineapple motif on each side. Decorative examples might be taken to a ball by a chaperone or lady's maid to pin up a flounce torn by the heavy step of a dancing partner. Some of these pin cushions might be trimmed with lace, as are many pincushions on lacemakers' pillows today.

A Victorian 'miser's purse' kept coins safe. This one is netted; others might be crochet, knitting or beadwork. Sometimes the two tassels differed so the owner could tell by feel which end had copper coins, and which silver, allowing easy selection of the right coin when making a payment in low light.

You want to make it difficult for anyone to get at the coins in your purse? So you crochet one with a criss-cross of chains that allows coins to be easily dropped in, but fiddly to get out.

Crochet is probably the most versatile of the craft laces for producing small items, but other techniques can be found, for example this tatted bag, just 18cm high.

Little crochet baskets were hung beside a dressing table to take long hairs from the hairbrush after the daily brushing. Courtesy Sheila Priestly.

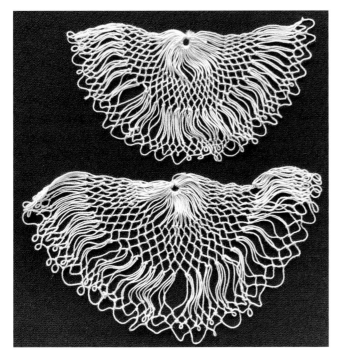

Puzzle pieces: some items might sit in a collection for years before there is any answer to the question 'what was this for?' The answer may come if you see something similar or look at a piece in a different way – often it is a case of waiting until you ask the right question of the right person. In this case it was Gwynedd Roberts, honorary curator at The Lace Guild who discovered the purpose of these netted semicircles (5.5cm and 6.5cm radius). She had seen similar items in a little museum in France dedicated to filet. There they were described as dress ornaments – in the 1920s they were stitched in pairs to the skirt of a flapper dress to swing as a fringe as the owner danced.

In the 1960s and '70s, many lacemakers moved away from traditional style lace for household and fashion items and towards pictorial and sculptural items such as this bobbin lace piece worked in silver and gold thread with wire and beads.

Doll and dolls' house enthusiasts often make or buy small-scale lace for clothes and furnishings. More often than not the lace is machine made, occasionally it is scraps of vintage or even eighteenth-century lace, or it may be hand-made for a specific purpose, such as these Torchon cushions and sofa back – the latter the only antimacassar in our collections – a 1/12 scale version of a 1950s example in the York Castle museum.

Flowers and Butterflies

Flowers and leaves are popular motifs in many styles of lace, particularly Honiton, and other pieced bobbin laces, and free-flowing needle laces such as Point de Gaze. Butterflies are less common, but are often there. Today many three-dimensional examples can be found of individual flowers, small posies and corsages made entirely of lace, and there are even a few complete bouquets – usually made as a group project. There are three main types of three-dimensional lace flower: those made from gathered edgings; close copies in simple bobbin lace of actual flowers assembled from individual petals; and fantasy flowers where anything goes.

The small wooden vase has delicate flowers assembled from individual leaves and petals. The second vase was a table decoration at a North American lace convention. In this the flowers are composed of gathered Torchon edgings.

The butterfly is three-dimensional, composed of two layers of chemical lace, with a brooch pin. Bought in Belgium as a souvenir gift

Earrings and Necklaces

The increasing use of lace techniques to make jewellery has been a feature of the past quarter century. Small items such as earrings, made either with wire or with thread which is later stiffened, are particularly popular.

The earrings on the left are bobbin lace with beads, the ones on the right are needlelace worked with a variegated thread in autumn colours

This set of necklace and earrings is typical of the style of bobbin lace made popular by contemporary designers in Eastern Europe, particularly those in the Czech Republic. These pieces are worked in half stitch using different thicknesses of silver thread.

Bookmarks

In the days when women were trying to make a living from their lacemaking, a lacemaker in Devon might complete a lace sprig, carefully remove it from her pillow and place it between the pages of her Bible to press it flat and keep it clean. She might then send a child with the Bible to the village shop where the shopkeeper, who was also the middleman for a local lace dealer, would exchange the sprig for a small amount of food or other necessities.

Today if we find lace in a book it is more likely to have been put there to mark a place and since the resurgence of interest in lacemaking in the 1970s lace bookmarks have been popular projects for new and experienced lacemakers, either as gifts, or to try out new techniques and colour combinations.

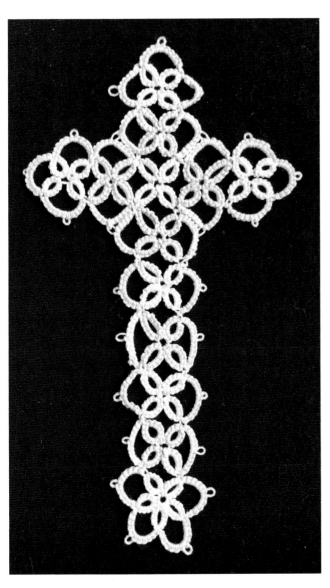

A small tatted bookmark composed of simple rings and chains, worked in two colours which would have required the use of two shuttles, one with white thread, one with yellow.

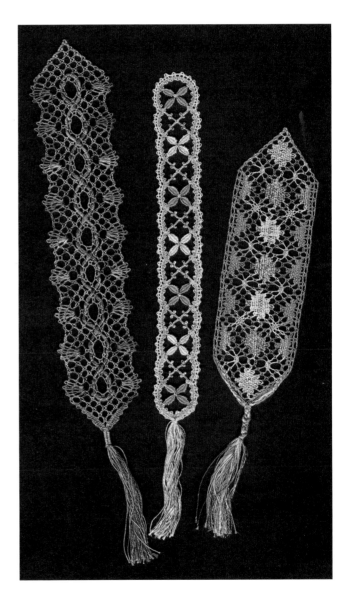

Trio of bobbin-lace bookmarks using two or more colours. The bookmark in the centre is Bedfordshire; the others are Torchon.

Remodel and Re-Use

For much of its history lace has been a highly valued textile and therefore remodelled and re-used as fashions changed or when the lace got damaged. Lace from several different sources may be put together, sometimes assembled with a considerable amount of care, in other cases roughly stitched together by someone who clearly knew little about the lace they were handling.

In the second half of the twentieth century, patchwork lace began to be marketed as Normandy lace. This was usually composed of fairly large pieces of machine lace assembled as tablecloths, bedspreads and other household items. This type of patchwork is also made domestically, often recycling scraps and larger pieces from the maker's collection. Patchwork lace made at the end of the nineteenth century was usually composed of heavier laces, sometimes including both seventeenth-century guipures (needle and bobbin made) and nineteenth-century reproductions. This type of lace is one of the many that have been called Greek lace.

A contemporary take on Normandy patchwork lace is this colourful fan, titled *From Dusk to Dawn*, designed and made by Deborah Robinson using sections of machine-made guipure laces.

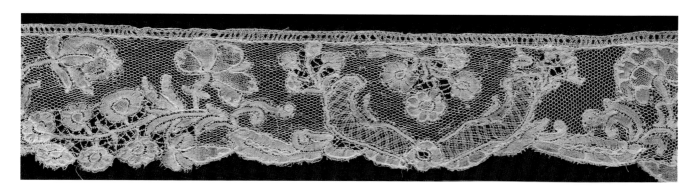

It is not immediately obvious that this is a patchwork. It appears as a pieced bobbin lace with a mesh background, but a closer look reveals a number of features that show it has been assembled from small pieces from several sources that were made in different centuries. The first clue is that the rather crude engrelure cuts through the motifs along the upper edge. The motifs themselves are of different styles, some carefully worked with raised outline, others flat and amorphous in shape. The real surprise is the ground: on the left is the bobbin-made Droschel ground which was used extensively in the eighteenth century for Honiton lace, while on the right is a small area of machine-made bobbinet.

Sample Books

There are many reasons for collecting lace samples. In the nineteenth century they were assembled by dealers to show what laces were available. The Lace Guild has one of these sample books from the Winslow Lace Industry – established in Buckinghamshire by the Hubbard family in 1875 and providing work for many lacemakers in and around the town of Winslow. A rather larger collection of samples is in the Luton Museum; these were collected between 1820 and 1900 from a number of sources. The samples are now mounted on thirty-three A3 pages, with between twenty and eighty samples per page; eight of the pages have examples of Bedfordshire lace (collected after 1850), the rest are point ground.

Collecting lace samples to mount in an elaborate album was a popular hobby for ladies at the end of the nineteenth century. The pieces collected were usually quite small, often no more than one repeat, and the information alongside is not always accurate and rarely gives details of where the lace was acquired. A small lace museum in Sunnyvale California has one of these collections, and intriguingly one of the pieces seems to have been cut from the same length of lace as a piece in an album in the Lace Guild's collection, while another piece in the museum exactly matches a length in an album owned by a lady living near Durham in northern England.

Individuals wanting to record the lace they make often assemble an album or file of samples for their own interest or to present work for assessment. These samples may be supported by background information such as pattern source, techniques and threads used.

This sample roll is probably one person's work. It was given to Gil's mother when she was a child in Evesham in about 1926. The lace is a mix of Cluny and Torchon techniques.

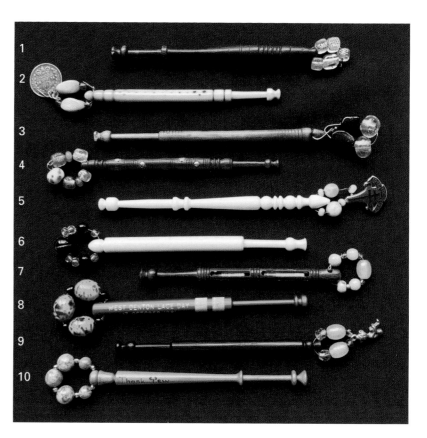

Spangled English bobbins, average length 10cm + spangle

1. Nineteenth-century wood with its original spangle of handmade beads.

2. Nineteenth-century bone, re-spangled in the twentieth century with 1875 coin.

3. Nineteenth-century fruit-wood with the original spangle attached by a twisted pin.

4. Nineteenth-century with pewter spots, known as a leopard bobbin.

5. Late twentieth-century plastic bobbin copied from a turned wooden bobbin.

6. Bone bobbin from catalogue of John Harris and Sons.

7. Mother-and-babe bobbin with inserts of tiny bobbins.

8. Aluminium bobbin, one of a series produced by Sebalace in the 1980s.

9. Simple turned wood with a spangle of amber beads and Lincoln Imp charm.

10. Yew wood bobbin by Derrick Earnshaw with his trademark handbell at the end.

Lace-Related Items

When you are looking for lace you may also come across a variety of lacemaking equipment. The most obvious items are the bobbins. Particularly attractive are the East Midlands bobbins, with their ring of coloured beads (known as spangles) and sometimes an inscription. Contrary to popular belief lacemakers do not look at their bobbins as they work – the beads provide weight and the different colours and patterns are purely decorative, while inscriptions may record mementos of family members, or local or national events. When lace was being made for sale in the nineteenth century there was only one small area of England – the counties of Bedfordshire, Buckinghamshire and Northamptonshire – where spangled bobbins were used, but they are now popular in many parts of the world. Most bobbins are made of wood, some are bone (rarely if ever ivory since most lacemakers came from poor communities). Glass and metal bobbins can be found and increasingly ones made of plastic or other synthetic materials, with some experiments being made with three-dimensional printing. Be careful when buying second-hand bobbins, some plastic ones can look remarkably like wooden or bone ones

– look out for raised lines that are remnants of the moulding process.

Early in the twentieth century a major supplier of bobbins, threads and other lacemaking equipment was John Harris and Sons, based in Cockermouth from 1893 to 1934. The company offered a mail order service with special terms for Mission schools and lace industries. Some of their bobbins were made in France, others in the UK and many of the bobbins turn up on pillows and in collections today. Braggins of Bedford were also selling lacemaking equipment and continued to do so until the 1970s. Many of the Braggins bobbins were recycled from the nineteenth century. As the interest in bobbin lace gathered pace in the 1970s a number of wood turners rose to the challenge of supplying bobbins to the new hobby lacemakers. A few bobbin makers and painters of bobbins were able to turn their hobby into a business, often producing sets of bobbins – different woods, historic figures, birds, flowers and so on – which has encouraged lacemakers to become bobbin collectors as well. The work of a number of nineteenth- and late twentieth-century bobbin lacemakers can be recognized by the distinctive shape of the head and/or the tail of the bobbin.

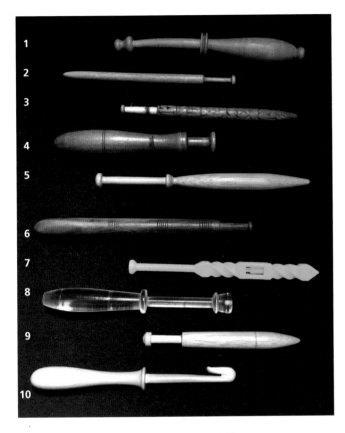

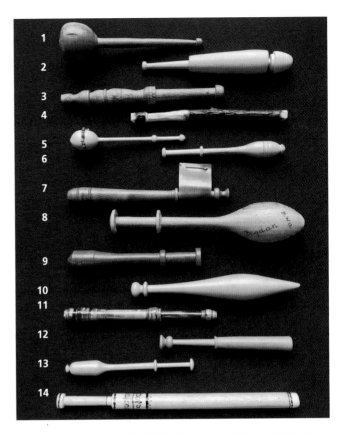

Unspangled English bobbins

1. Boxwood bobbin from John Harris, branch wood warped to this curve as it aged.
2. Lightweight Honiton bobbin for use with fine thread, pointed for easy sewings.
3. Unusual example of a Honiton bobbin with incised and coloured decoration.
4. South Bucks Thumper used for point ground.
5. Basic bobbin widely used in north-east England from the 1950s.
6. Malmesbury bobbin.
7. 3-D printed copy of a mother-and-babe bobbin, 2018.
8. Acrylic, turned by a lab technician who was also a lacemaker and teacher (lab technicians also made glass bobbins).
9. Downton bobbin.
10. Hook-head bobbin (10.5cm long) for metallic threads, the shape adapted by Derrick Earnshaw from large German bobbins used for working gold lace.

This is a small selection of bobbins from around the world. Most are traditional to the place in which they are used, appropriate for both the type of lace made and the pillow on which it is worked. These bobbins range in length from 9.5cm (Danish) to 18cm (Russian).

1. Portugal: similar bobbins are used in Brazil where the ball end might be a nut.
2. Germany: the loose cover acts as a handle and protects a large amount of thread.
3. Malta: quite rough when first made but become smooth with use.
4. Finland: traditionally whittled from the native silver birch, surprisingly comfortable to use.
5. Denmark; lightweight bobbin with tiny beads set in a groove in the handle.
6. Belgium: one of many styles designed to roll across the pillow.
7. France: this one still has a parchment cover for the wound thread.
8. Poland: most Polish laces use few bobbins so there is room on large pillows for bulky bobbins.
9. India: early example of recycled plastic (2002), comfortable for working Torchon and Cluny.
10. Italy: a good shape for working Cantu lace on a tombola pillow.
11. Luxemburg: rolled and varnished magazine pages; similar paper bobbins are made elsewhere.
12. Spain; often made of olive wood, bobbins of this shape are traditional in several countries.
13. Belgian style: made in England.
14. Russia: for braid lace needing lots of sewings, worked on large pillows.

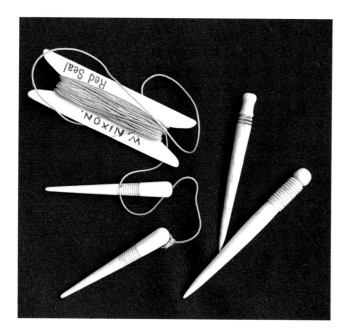

Many tools for craft laces can be found in old workboxes, often alongside other small items that have nothing to do with any form of textile craft. This can create a considerable puzzle. For example, bone, wood or ivory stilettos are used by embroiderers to make the small holes in fabric for Broderie Anglaise and Ayrshire whitework. Sometimes the stiletto has a hole which can be threaded with a cord and hung round the neck so the tool is always to hand. The two stilettos on the right of this picture have no holes, the two on the left do and are attached to a long length of cord. It took many months to discover that, although they were found in a workbox, these have absolutely nothing to do with any form of craft. They are actually used by bowlers to compare the distance from the jack of two competing bowls.

Old bobbin lace patterns, pricked on parchment may occasionally be found. The ones here have been rolled up for storage and would need careful unrolling and pressing under weights or in a trouser press before the design could be seen with any ease. Some prickings have strips of strong linen (known as eches) stitched to the ends; these were pinned firmly to the pillow to keep the pattern in place for working. Attached to one of these prickings is a small sample of lace – a useful reference to the lace that could be worked on that pricking.

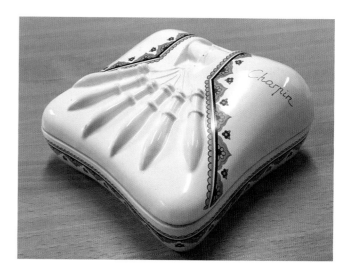

This little tool is one of the patented gadgets for making small circles in Tenerife lace. The spokes are prepared by winding thread around the cogs and when the circle is finished the supporting strut is unclipped and the disc folded, which allows the lace to be easily lifted off.

A friend in France found this ceramic box shaped like a French lace pillow, complete with bobbins and a narrow piece of lace. From contact with lacemakers around the world we have located four similar boxes and discovered that they were originally filled with chocolates, and were sold in Le Puy, the centre of a lacemaking area in France.

Small hooks are among the most common items to be found in workboxes, they are used in many textile crafts in addition to crochet lace: sewings in bobbin lace and tatting; finishing a piece of knitted lace; working a border around machine lace; making tambour lace; mending stockings and other knitted items… Most of the small hooks are steel, and they may have bone, wood or plastic handles, occasionally ivory and there were many patented designs such as the one at the top of the picture. The small hooks in this collection are stored in a wooden box, which had an earlier life as a spectacle case. The other tools are tatting shuttles: two late twentieth-century plastic ones (on left), a bone one from early in the century and a modern wooden one.

My friend in France also sent this, saying: 'The wooden thingy is for Jean. I found it in a *brocante* and just wonder if it could have been used in lacemaking?' (A *brocante* is a second-hand shop or flea market.) Some online research revealed that it was in fact a *broche* used in gold thread embroidery, with the slit at the end holding the thread so it wasn't tarnished by contact with the fingers.

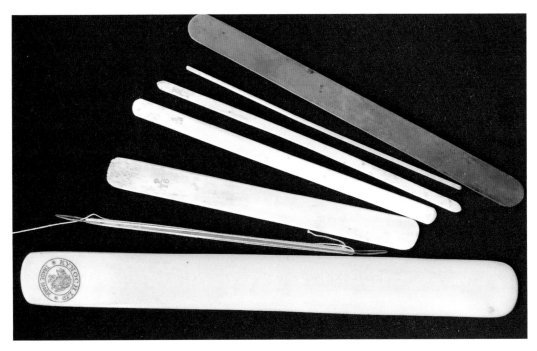

Most of the items in this group are for netting. There is a steel needle (shuttle) for holding the thread and three bone mesh sticks marked with their sizes: 3/16, 5/16 and 9/16 of an inch (there was probably a 7/16 stick in the original set). It is possible that the very slim bone stick is also a gauge of some sort, but it is too short to be part of this set and may be too fine for netting, so for the moment this remains a puzzle piece. There is a larger item that looks like a bone mesh stick, but researching the trademark Kynoch Ltd shows it is a letter opener (which also works well for producing sharp creases in paper or card). It was made in the mid-twentieth century as a promotional item for a company that manufactured ammunition. Bone always has brownish marks within the cream and the absence of any such marks in this piece indicates that it is not bone. It is in fact celluloid – which has many of the same chemical components as the explosive nitrocellulose. The metal strip could be used as a mesh stick, but it is more than likely it had a completely different purpose – it is quite flexible so was possibly once part of the boning of a corset.

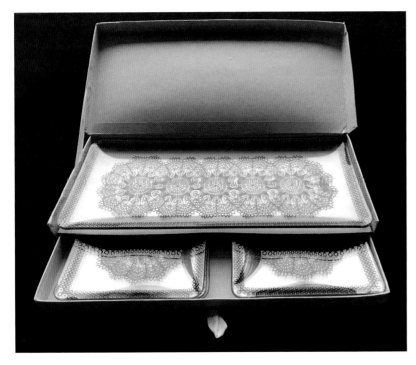

A final lace-related oddity in our collections is this set of glass tray and dishes bought second hand in the 1990s. A similar tray but with white knitted lace was for sale online described as 'Holland lace bought in Holland as a holiday souvenir in 1970'. Annoyingly the label on this box is torn and shows only the word 'glass' and two tiny dancers – the clothes the dancers are wearing could be Dutch so there seems no reason to suppose that this set is not also Dutch. The design for the tray appears to be printed within the glass from a pattern that has been 'cut and pasted' from a single knitted disc, the same disc that is used in the dishes. Tray is 15cm × 35cm.

GLOSSARY

Appliqué – Applying fabric (including lace) to the surface of another fabric.

Artificial silk – A thread spun from cellulose, usually wood pulp, also known as rayon.

Bars – Links between two areas of lace: made of twisted, plaited, looped or stitched threads.

Bobbin – Handle on which thread is wound for working bobbin lace.

Bobbin lace – Lace made with multiple threads, each held on a bobbin for working.

Bobbinet – Machine-made net with a hexagonal mesh.

Bone-lace – An early name for bobbin lace.

Border – Lace attached to a fabric edge, a wide edging; also decoration at the edge of other laces.

Braid – A narrow structure of closely worked threads.

Buttonhole stitch – The basic stitch used in needle lace.

Casket – An enclosed area within a piece of lace.

Chemical lace – Machine-embroidered lace worked on a background that is chemically removed.

Cloth stitch – Basic bobbin lace stitch that looks like woven cloth.

Clothwork – Close work in a piece of lace.

Couching – Stitching a thread to the surface of lace or other fabric.

Couronne – A small ring, usually of needle lace.

Crochet – Technique for producing fabric from a single thread using a hand-held hook.

Crochet cotton – A firm, rounded thread made by twisting together three 2-ply threads.

Drawn thread work – A form of open-work embroidery where threads are withdrawn from the fabric.

Edging – Lace stitched to the edge of fabric.

Embroidery – Decorative stitches worked with a sewing needle.

Engrelure – A length of narrow lace (usually machine made) attached to the straight edge of a lace.

Fan – Scallop shapes along a headside.

Filet – A knotted net.

Filling – Stitches within a motif.

Floater – A thread that is carried from one area of a design to the next, usually cut off later.

Footside – Straight edge of lace to attach to a fabric.

Gimp – An outlining thread in bobbin lace.

Grounds – The stitch combinations that make up the background to many laces.

Guipure – Lace without a net background.

Headside – The edge of a lace that hangs free.

Insertion – Lace with two straight edges that can join two pieces of fabric.

Lace runners – People employed to put outlining threads into machine-patterned nets and lace.

Linen – Thread spun from flax, in some contexts any thread that is not silk; fabric made from linen.

Liner – Outline thread in machine lace.

Motif – Element of a design.

Needle lace – Lace made with a needle and single thread, a form of free embroidery.

Needle-run – Stitching a thread in and out of net (running stitch).

Net – A machine-made mesh; or a knotted fabric similar in structure to fishing net.

Plait – In bobbin lace, four threads worked together.

Picot – A small decorative loop.

Pieced lace – Lace assembled from separate motifs.

Pillow lace – Another name for bobbin lace.

Point – Literally 'stitch', but also any fine lace, and part of other names such as Point de Gaze.

Pricking – Card or parchment pattern for bobbin lace, with holes where pins will be placed.

Provenance – The known history of an item.

Russian stitch – An embroidery stitch worked across a gap, similar to herringbone stitch.

Silk – Yarn twisted or spun from filaments produced by the silk moth.

Spider – A lace feature consisting of 'legs' and a solid central area.

Sprig – Small motif.

Tally – Generic name for a small woven block found in bobbin lace and machine-made imitations.

Tambour – Chain stitch worked with a hook on fabric or net.

Tape lace – Lace based on machine-made tapes.

Thread – Any yarn used for making lace (until the 1950s it meant linen, not silk or other fibre).

Thread lace – Lace made with linen thread.

Whipping – Wrapping a thread around another thread, or group of threads.

TIME LINE

1760–1830: Gradual improvement of machine spinning of cotton

1764: Plain knitted net from modified stocking frame, needle-run decoration

1765: Patterned net with hand run outlines

1786: Point-net, six-sided knitted mesh

1800s: Lightweight dresses, high waistline, frills at neck and bottom of skirt, little lace

1808: John Heathcoat's twist-net machine imitating point ground, just 1in (2.5cm) wide

1809: Wide bobbinet; major industry in Nottingham, Ireland, Switzerland and Austria

1813: John Leavers' modified twist-net machine

1820: Carrickmacross made in Ireland

1820s: Experiments with sewing machines: Bonnaz, Cornely

1829: Tambour moved from Essex to Ireland

1830: Pusher machine

1834: Jacquard cards

1840: Queen Victoria's wedding, brief revival of Honiton lace

1840s: Potato blight, famine in Ireland, Irish crochet

1841: Possible to work in outline threads in machine lace: end of need for lace-runners

1846: Curtain-lace machine, square mesh

1850s: Peak of handmade lace production running alongside explosion of machine lace

1851: Great Exhibition recorded lace designers, manufactures and hand workers

1859: Raschel machine, double warp knitting

1860s: Loss of American market due to Civil War

1861: Death of Prince Albert, demand for black lace

1865: Schiffli embroidery machine imitating almost every type of lace (chemical lace)

1867: Workshop Act, no child under eight to be employed in handicrafts

1870: Education Act, all children to age of ten had to go to school

1860–1880: Slump in demand due to wars

1880: Lace trimmings back in fashion

1875–1900: Arts and Crafts movement

1890: Barmen machine

1890s: Artificial silk

1900: Art Nouveau

1903: Start of the Suffragette movement

1914–18: First World War

1938: Nylon

1939–45: Second World War

1951: Polyester

1983: Computer-controlled Raschel machine

1995: Lace on the internet, including dedicated websites and discussion groups

RESOURCES

Over the past five centuries lace has played a major role in many aspects of life and has been written about extensively in books and pamphlets and now online. It is not always easy to sort fact from fantasy, and family tradition cannot always be relied upon, but the resources listed below will build on the information supplied in this book.

Books

Overall view of lace including pre-1800

Caulfield, S.F.A and Saward, B.C, *Dictionary of Needlework* (first published 1882). A fascinating collection of instructions for working a wide range of textile crafts together with information about materials and tools, sometimes including prices.

Earnshaw, Pat, *Bobbin and Needle Laces: Identification and Care* (Batsford 1983)

Earnshaw, Pat, *Threads of Lace from Source to Sink* (Gorse Publications 1989)

Levey, Santina, *Lace: A History* (V&A 1983)

McFadzean, Carol, *Mrs Treadwin: Victorian Lacemaker, Designer and Historian* (Carol McFadzean 2009)

Simeon, Margaret, *The History of Lace* (Stainer and Bell 1979)

Toomer, Heather, *Lace: A Guide to Identification of Old Lace Types and Techniques* (Batsford 1989)

Fashion

Buck, Anne, *Victorian Costume and Costume Accessories* (Ruth Bean 1984, and earlier editions)

Buck, Anne, *Clothes and the Child* (Ruth Bean 1996)

Earnshaw, Pat, *Lace in Fashion from the Sixteenth to the Twentieth Century* (Batsford 1985)

Peacock, John, *Costume 1066 to the Present Day* (Thames and Hudson 2006), sketches of clothes.

Wardle, Patricia, *Victorian Lace* (Ruth Bean 1982, and earlier editions)

Machine lace

Earnshaw, Pat, *Lace Machines and Machine Laces* (Batsford 1986)

Lowe, David and Richards, Jack, *The City of Lace* (Nottingham Lace Centre 1982)

Handmade laces

Blanchard, Joan, *Malmesbury Lace* (Batsford 1990)

Bryson, Agnes F., *Ayrshire Needlework* (Batsford 1989)

Buck, Anne, *Thomas Lester, His Lace and the East Midlands Industry* (Ruth Bean 1981)

Dudding, Jean, *Creating Coggeshall Lace* (Jean Dudding 1994)

Earnshaw, Pat, *Needlelace* (Merehurst 1991)

Howener-Townsend, Nicky, *Suffolk Lace and the Lacemakers of Eye* (self published 2009)

Kaspian, Alice Odion, *Armenian Needlelace and Embroidery* (EPM Publications 1983)

Kemp, Bertha, *Downton Lace* (Dryad 1988)

Kieboom, Ineke van den, *The Technique of Tape Lace* (Batsford 1994)

Konior, Mary, *Heritage Crochet: An Analysis* (Dryad 1987)

Laurie, M. and Meldrum, A., *The Borris Lace Collection* (Sally Milner Publishing 2010)

Luxton, Elsie, *The Technique of Honiton Lace* (Batsford 1979)

Nicholls, Elgiva, *Tatting, Technique and History* (Longacre Press 1962)

Niven, Mary, *Flanders Lace* (Dryad 1988)

Nottingham, Pamela, *The Technique of Bucks Point Lace* (Batsford 1981)

O Cléirigh, Nellie, *Carrickmacross Lace* (Dolman/Dryad 1985)

OIDFA Study Group, *Point Ground Lace, a Comparative Study* (OIDFA 2001)

Prickett, Elizabeth, *Ruskin Lace and Linen Work* (Batsford 1985)

Read, Patricia and Kincaid, Lucy, *New Braids and Designs in*

Milanese Lace (Batsford 1994)

Skovgaard, Inge, *The Technique of Tønder Lace* (Batsford 1991)

Trivett, Lillie D., *The Technique of Branscombe Point* (Batsford 1991)

Underwood, Barbara M., *Traditional Bedfordshire Lace* (Ruth Bean 1988)

Bobbins

Springett, Christine and David, *Success to the Lace Pillow* (C&D Springett 1997)

Museums

These British museums are known to have lace collections where at least some of the identification and supporting information has been prepared by curators or volunteers with good lace knowledge. Relatively little lace may be on display, but information and images may be available online and it may be possible to book an appointment to view selected items.

Allhallows Museum
High St, Honiton, EX14 1PG

Bowes Museum
Barnard Castle, County Durham, DL12 8NP

Burrell Collection
Pollokshaws Road, Pollok Country Park, Glasgow, G43 1AT

Discovery Museum
Blandford Square, Newcastle upon Tyne, NE1 4JA

Fashion Museum
Assembly Rooms, Bennet Street, Bath, BA1 2QH

The Higgins Art Gallery & Museum
Castle Lane, Bedford, MK40 3XD

The Lace Guild
The Hollies, 53 Audnam, Stourbridge, DY8 4AE

Museum of London
150 London Wall, London, EC2Y 5HN

National Museum of Scotland
Chambers St, Edinburgh, EH1 1JF

Nottingham Castle, Museum and Art Gallery
Lenton Road, Nottingham NG1 6EL

Royal Albert Memorial Museum
Queen Street, Exeter, EX4 3RX

Rachel Kay-Shuttleworth Collection
Gawthorpe Hall, Burnley Road, Padiham (near Burnley, Lancs.), BB12 8UA

Victoria &Albert Museum
Cromwell Road, London, SW7 2RL

Wardown House Museum
Old Bedford Road, Luton, LU2 7HA

Web and Digital

DATS Toolkits
www.dressandtextilespecialists.org.uk
Produced for museum specialists, it has downloadable booklets on *Identifying Handmade Lace* (includes conservation, storage and display of lace) and *Identifying Handmade and Machine Lace.*

Care of lace
http://www.honitonlace.com/honitonlace/shop/cleaning2.htm
A practical guide to the cleaning of lace: what to do, and more importantly what not to do, when caring for lace in your collection.
http://www.textilerestoration.co.uk/
Supplier of conservation services and specialist products for the care of historic textiles.

Art UK
artuk.org
The online home for public art collections in the UK. Many of the portraits give an indication of the lace worn as 'best dress' by the middle classes and aristocracy.

Gilian Dye
www.gilslacemiscellany.com
A collection of material based on Gil's research into her many areas of lace interest.

Jean Leader
www.jeanleader.net
Information about Jean's lace, teaching, books and videos.
www.lacetypes.com
A historical guide to European laces.
Lace – iPhone and iPad app
A quick reference to lace styles. Available from the iOS App store, further information at www.jeanleader.net/publications/lace-app.html

INDEX